The Life & Legacy of Bill Daniels

The Life & Legacy
of
Bill Daniels

ISBN 978-0-9835637-2-3
produced by:
Tell Studios Inc.
www.TellStudios.com

Cover and Book Design by Nikki Ward, Morrison Alley Design
Front cover photograph by Nicholas DeSciose

Printed in the UNITED STATES OF AMERICA

CONTENTS

FOREWORD

The pages in this book hold more than just a story. It's a great one, without a doubt. But there's also a *reason* for this book, and sharing it with you now is our distinct pleasure.

There is, for each of us, a unique narrative to our lives: a record of who we are, what we stand for, and what we do about it. It is a tally of the ways we forever change, and are changed by, the billions of lives unfolding with ours.

Remarkably, exceptionally few strike us as "larger than life," often for reasons that elude explanation. When a person such as this comes to the end of his or her journey, there remains an opportunity to preserve an important story. The reason is surprisingly simple: The knowledge and inspiration offered by a remarkable life story need to be preserved so they can brighten the paths of those still being written.

Bill Daniels was, undeniably, larger than life. He stood tall among us, achieving great heights, not on the backs of others, but with the reach of those he helped to climb. He was guided by principles and values that too often seem rare. Bill was also just a man: a human being, far from perfect, and no stranger to mistakes. Bill learned from his experiences and he allowed his compassion for others to shape him. He leveraged his intellect, instinct, and a healthy dose of luck to construct a new industry, earning a fortune in the process.

Nearly all of us knew Bill Daniels and were fortunate to be a part of his larger-than-life journey. Some of us worked by his side as he made his mark in business. Some assisted him as he changed lives with his philanthropy. Others were involved in his political endeavors. We continue to learn from Bill to this very day. As these words are being written, it's been more than 12 years since Bill passed away. Our feelings for him have faded not one bit. Because of Bill's legacy, now in our care, neither has he.

The Daniels Fund carries forward Bill Daniels' legacy of generosity. In his final years, he laid the plans for the foundation that would bear his name. He defined the scope and method and impact of its philanthropy. We are united in our commitment to honor Bill's wishes with fidelity. Any individual generous enough to leave the rewards of their work as a gift to the community deserves nothing less. That's why for nearly two years, we combed through tens of thousands of items — Bill's own correspondence, photos, videos, print and television coverage, interviews, documents of every kind — to bring you Bill's story. We want you to know him, too. You'll notice how the Daniels Fund and its efforts look and feel like the man who built them.

With this book, it is our goal to motivate and guide future board members and associates in their privilege and obligation as caretakers of Bill's legacy to honor his intent.

The Daniels Fund Board of Directors
August 2012

Hank Brown, Chairman

Linda Childears, President and CEO

Tony Acone

Brian Deevy

Francisco Garcia

Gayle Greer

Jim Griesemer

Tom Marinkovich

Jim Nicholson

Dan Ritchie

June Travis

ACKNOWLEDGMENTS

Writing a book is in some ways like starting and running a company. Success depends a great deal on many people, who all contribute their unique talents toward a common goal. We are deeply indebted to all of them.

First and foremost, we thank our exceptional editorial committee at the Daniels Fund who worked so enthusiastically with us to make sure that we captured a true picture of Bill Daniels and the huge impact he had on the Daniels Fund, the community, and the world. Our heartfelt thanks go to Linda Childears, Bo Peretto, Dale Bradley, and Peter Droege. Their enthusiasm and passion for the project were inspirational. It was a genuine pleasure and privilege to work with them.

We're also grateful to Bill's friends and Daniels Fund board members who read the manuscript and offered their suggestions and encouragement: Hank Brown, John Saeman, and June Travis.

We extend special thanks to Stephanie Kadel Taras, a gifted writer and true friend, for the talents and insight she brought to this project.

Finally, without the efforts and encouragement of Don Richards, we might never have had this unique opportunity to preserve Bill Daniels' life and legacy. He believed so much in Tell Studios and the value of our work that he introduced us to Linda Childears and championed our working relationship.

Jeanne S. Archer
Andy Archer
Tell Studios Inc.
August 2012

PART ONE

BILL DANIELS' LIFE STORY

CHAPTER ONE

WHO WAS BILL DANIELS?

I've lived a fantastic life. I've had a ball. I've done everything that a guy could want to do . . . I've got all the money I could ever spend. To me, the excitement is: What's next? What contribution can we make? That's where all the fun is.

~ Bill Daniels

PHOTO BY NICHOLAS DESCIOSE

When Bill Daniels entered the world on July 1, 1920, no one other than his devoted mother could have imagined how many lives would be made better through his vision, perseverance, and hard work. Over the course of his lifetime, he served his country as a fighter pilot in two wars, became a pioneer in an

Bill smiles in this photograph, taken in 1985.

industry that changed the way that people communicate, and contributed millions of dollars to deserving people and worthy causes.

As a role model and mentor to many, Bill often encouraged others to take a chance on themselves — to have the courage to try something new and see what was possible, for themselves and for society.

His advice was born of experience. Most of his ventures turned out well. However, this driven, dynamic visionary would be the first to admit that he also took chances that were not so successful. But Bill learned lessons from each venture, and he kept moving forward. And in his later years, when young executives and college students and entrepreneurs turned to him for advice, he had a lifetime of hard-won wisdom to share.

From his humble beginnings growing up poor in Depression-era America to his last days as a successful trailblazer in a booming industry, Bill witnessed change at lightning speed, both in the country he loved as well as in his own life. Yet he found that the same values and behaviors that he learned growing up served him well as a business and community leader.

He held himself and others to high standards and, by doing so, inspired and motivated others to succeed. In short, he brought out the best in people by believing in them and in what they were accomplishing together. While Bill's career changed the world, his philanthropy will continue to change lives for generations.

As visitors enter the Denver headquarters of the Daniels Fund, they pass a larger-than-life sculpture of Bill Daniels. He sits at ease with his hands folded. His lips, curved into a slight smile, hint at a sense of humor. His eyes seem to observe those who pass through the main doors of the Daniels Fund. Over his shoulder is the headquarters of Young Americans Bank, the only bank in the world exclusively for kids. Starting it was one of Bill's proudest achievements.

The statue was a gift to the Daniels Fund from a former publisher in the cable industry who lost everything to bankruptcy in the late 1980s. After all other avenues had failed, he sought help from Bill Daniels, who agreed to give his industry colleague an unsecured loan large enough to help him get a fresh start. Ultimately, the man was not able to repay the loan during his benefactor's lifetime.

In 2005, five years after Bill's death, the Daniels Fund was considering options for creating some kind of permanent tribute to its founder. Then, unexpectedly, the former publisher emerged with an offer to cover the cost of a bronze sculpture as a way to honor the memory of the man who had taken a chance on him. Even though the loan had long been forgotten, the man indebted to Bill said he felt compelled to do this because it was the kind of thing he knew Bill Daniels would have done.

The sculpture doesn't just immortalize a man; it immortalizes his legacy and the foundation he endowed to serve the needs of people in Colorado, New Mexico, Utah, and Wyoming. His presence is larger than life for the many people who knew him and wanted to remember him with this book.

Throughout his professional life, Bill Daniels was interviewed by reporters all around the world and gave speeches to thousands who hung on his every word. The articles acknowledge Bill's role in revolutionizing the cable television industry, report on his sports franchises, and honor his philanthropic generosity. But for all the accolades he received in his lifetime, Bill never forgot that relationships are built *one person at a time*.

One way that he built and sustained lasting relationships was through letter writing. These letters, *in his own words*, give a deeper understanding of the man, revealing his emotions, personality, and care for others. Bill's immense body of correspondence is a treasure and a reminder of one of the hallmarks of his life: communication, communication, communication.

With a secretary to do the typing, he sent thousands of letters over the years and kept copies, many of which still exist. Bill used correspondence for much more than keeping up with old friends.

Bill's prompt and frequent correspondence — which often contained advice and encouragement — became legendary. He clipped articles to send to his associates and sent framed photographs to friends after they had visited him. He was vigilant about sending thank-you notes and wrote out-of-the-blue letters of appreciation to current or former associates just to let them know they were on his mind.

He wrote letters of congratulations when he saw someone's good news in the paper. He wrote letters of welcome to new associates in his company, espousing his core values: ethics, integrity, and compassion. He wrote to political leaders to remind them of the jobs they were elected to do, and he wrote to famous athletes to thank them for being good role models. He wrote to children to praise their good report cards and admonish bad behavior. He wrote to the mothers of his associates to thank them for their good parenting. He wrote to college students with encouragement and career advice. He wrote to new business owners to wish them good luck. He wrote to prisoners and ambassadors, reporters and college presidents, cadets in military school, and old Navy buddies. Bill was still writing letters just days before his death.

The following pages use many of Bill's own words to communicate his story and the values he hoped to share.

Renowned sculptor Kenneth Bunn created this sculpture of Bill, which sits in front of the Daniels Fund headquarters in Denver.

CHAPTER TWO

HARD WORK, PERSEVERANCE, AND MANNERS: A DEPRESSION-ERA CHILDHOOD

My mother used to tell people what a gentleman I had turned out to be, and that made up for everything else she had to put up with from me when I was a kid.

~ Bill Daniels

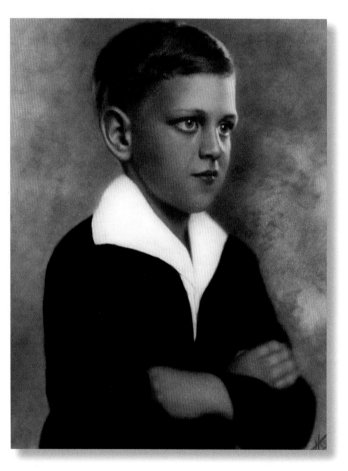

Bill Daniels learned his first lesson about business at the age of seven, when his father arrived home from work to find Bill and his four-year-old brother, Jack, running a lemonade stand in the front yard. They had sold a few nickel cups of lemonade to passersby and were excited to show their dad the coins they had accumulated.

"Good job, boys," their father said. "But don't forget that since you took the lemons and sugar from your mother's kitchen, you owe her four cents from every nickel you make."

Decades later, Bill joked that from then on, he learned to respect a 20 percent profit margin. He clearly learned to value work and wages. Most of what is known about Bill Daniels' early life has to do with jobs and money.

Born in Greeley, Colorado, Robert William "Bill" Daniels, Jr. was the third of four children of Adele Davis Daniels and Robert W. "Bob" Daniels. Bill's dad was born

When Bill squirmed as the photographer tried to take this photo, his mother asked him to "be good." With that, he crossed his arms and proclaimed, "I'm going to be the best at everything I do!"

Bill, at three months.

in Council Bluffs, Iowa, and his mother was from nearby Omaha, Nebraska. They were married in Omaha on October 23, 1915.

The young couple moved to Greeley after Bob got a sales job with a wholesale candy company. But when Bill was three, the family left Greeley for Omaha, where Bob became a life insurance salesman.

"My dad was a super salesman," Bill remembered. "One day my brother and I were outside in the woods, and our dog uncovered a $5 bill. My dad said the greatest selling job he ever did was talking us out of that five dollars. In those days that would fill a car with groceries."

Bob and Adele needed every dollar they could scrape together for their growing children — Bobette, Dorothy, Bill, and Jack — including the modest earnings from several peanut-vending machines Bob owned. Little Bill rode around Omaha with his dad to refill these machines, which dispensed a handful of peanuts for a penny. Bill began to earn his own money at age eight, when he got his first job selling the *The Saturday Evening Post* and *Liberty Magazine* door-to-door.

All these efforts could not stave off the effects of the Great Depression, however. When Bill was about 10 and the income from his father's insurance business could no longer cover the rent on their house, the family moved to Council Bluffs to live with Bob's mother.

Times were tough. Bill and Jack were sent out to gather wood from the nearby hills to feed the furnace. Adele sold 50-cent bottles of homemade rosewater lotion door-to-door. Bob continued to sell insurance but was often paid in chickens and eggs.

Both to help his family and to make a little spending money of his own, Bill began delivering newspapers and groceries. The summer he turned 12, he sold ice cream in

Bill knew a little about raising hell. Small but strong and tough as nails, he never backed away from a fight with other boys. "When we were kids," Bill's brother remembered, "I'd pick a fight, and Bill would jump in and try to take it over from me. He'd pop the guy before it got very far along. I guess you'd call that getting in the first lick. He was absolutely fearless. The bigger the guy — or the more of them — the better he liked it. If there were four of them and two of us, I could count on him to take three of them himself."

That relentless, tough, and aggressive attitude concerned Bill's parents, who became even more worried when he lost interest in excelling in school. He was clearly bright and self-motivated, but he lacked discipline.

Bill's mother took it upon herself to instruct her children in proper manners. One of five daughters of a doctor, Adele had attended finishing school in Boston and earned her teaching certificate at the University of Nebraska. As a refined and stylish woman, Adele expected her children to behave in public, to respect adults, and to know basic skills such as how to use the proper silverware at the dinner table. She taught her teenage sons to pull out a lady's chair at the table, stand when she entered a room, and escort her to the passenger door of a car.

Throughout his life, Bill gave thanks to his mother for teaching him manners. "My mother used to tell people what a gentleman I had turned out to be, and that made up for everything else she had to put up with from me when I was a kid."

In 1937, as Bill was finishing his second year of high school, Bob Daniels got an opportunity to run a statewide insurance agency out of Hobbs, New Mexico. He moved there in advance of the family and then sent for them to join him. Adele and the four kids took a train to Denver and then a bus to Clovis, New Mexico, where they arrived in the midst of a sandstorm so severe it made headlines in the papers.

Several more hours of driving on dirt roads brought them to Hobbs, a small oil-boom town with unpaved

Dixie cups from the back of his bicycle. "I bought them for a nickel and sold them for a dime," he said, "and I built up a good clientele."

Another job as a shoeshine boy in a hotel lobby led to a part-time bellhop position. At 16, Bill worked nights as a short-order cook in a hamburger stand. Although he hardly got enough sleep to stay awake in his high school classes, he liked the job because he could eat all the food he wanted.

The Daniels family attended the Episcopal church, where Bill was an altar boy and developed an early faith in God. But Bill sometimes went to the Catholic church with a childhood friend. "I would go with him to the Catholic church, so he could go to confession," Bill remembered. "Then we would come back and get on our bikes, and he would say, 'Let's raise hell for another week! I am cleansed, but you're not.' "

OPPOSITE | *Bill and his mother, Adele Davis Daniels.* ABOVE | *The four children of Adele and Bob Daniels were (from left) Bobette, Dorothy, Bill, and Jack.*

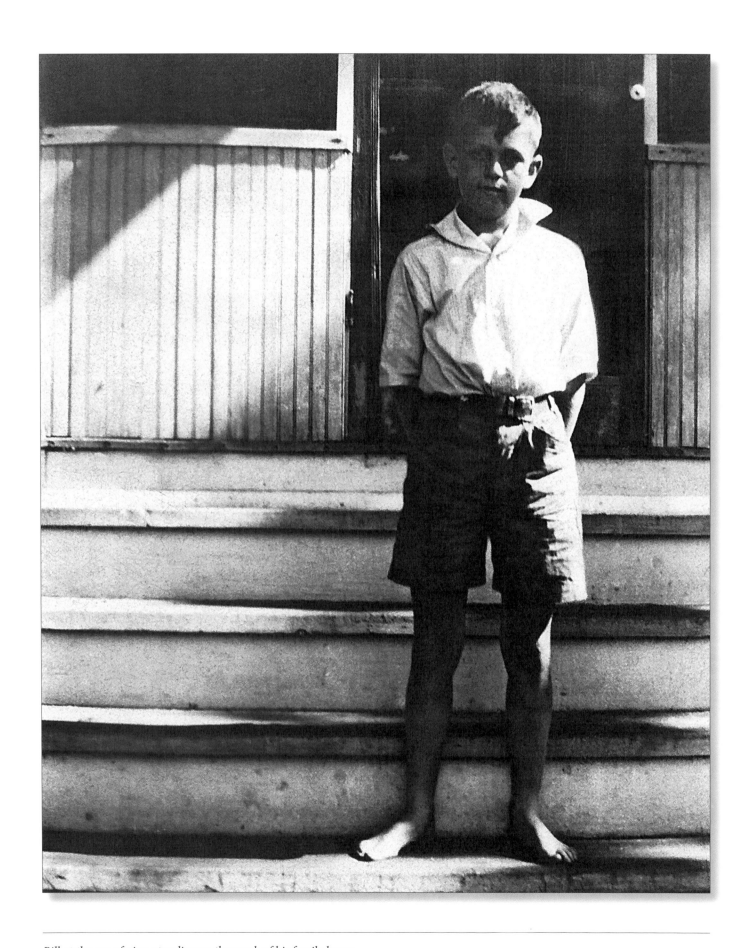

Bill at the age of nine, standing on the porch of his family home.

For all the city's potential, public schools in Hobbs in 1937 were not up to Adele's standards. She was especially anxious about Bill's education. The oldest Daniels child, Bobette, was 20 and out of the public school system when they arrived in Hobbs. Their next child, Dorothy, was mentally disabled and cared for by Adele at home. Jack, three years younger than Bill, was still in junior high. But Bill had two more years of high school to go, and he needed a school that would make the most of his energy and competitive nature.

Hobbs was a rough-and-tumble town that only seemed to encourage Bill's combative nature, and his parents were worried about his future. When Bob Daniels heard about the New Mexico Military Institute (NMMI), he decided to put his son on a bus to Roswell, New Mexico, and see if military school could straighten Bill out. "I was kind of a wild ass," Bill admitted bluntly, "so my dad sent me to NMMI."

roads, a couple of blocks of downtown buildings, dozens of oil rigs, and the dusty horizon visible in every direction. Adele, who would remain in Hobbs the rest of her life, never forgot her first impression of her new home. "We lived in a shotgun-style house in a town with not one tree in sight," she said.

The Daniels children didn't like Hobbs at first and wanted to return to their grandmother's house overlooking the river, but Bob and Adele talked to them about teamwork and the need to support one another. It was a good move for Bob, whose insurance company specializing in the oil industry grew to become one of the most successful insurance agencies in the state.

Bob and Adele quickly got involved in the community, including the local theater. Adele was a superb pianist who played by ear, and she and Bob both loved to sing and dance. They performed together at various gatherings. "They became a big hit in New Mexico," Bill remembered. "It was fun to watch them."

TOP | *Bill (at right) and his brother, Jack, pose with their father, Bob Daniels.* BOTTOM | *This photo of Bill was taken shortly before he left home to attend NMMI.*

CHAPTER THREE

DISCIPLINE, HONESTY, AND SECOND CHANCES: A YOUNG LEADER BEGINS TO EMERGE

I thought I was the toughest son of a bitch who ever came down the pike.
But, boy, did I find out in a hurry that I wasn't.

~ Bill Daniels

"I am far from perfect," Bill Daniels once wrote, "but had it not been for my time at NMMI, I would be *very, very, very* far from perfect."

Bill arrived at New Mexico Military Institute (NMMI) with a cardboard suitcase and a chip on his shoulder. "I thought I was the toughest son of a bitch who ever came down the pike," he remembered. "But, boy, did I find out in a hurry that I wasn't."

At the age of 17, Bill wasn't happy to be in military school, but he soon learned to thrive within its structure. He came to see close-order drill and formation as "the first step in basic discipline." He learned to be organized,

Bill with one of his fellow cadets at NMMI.

punctual, clean, and neat — virtues he tried to instill in others the rest of his life. He learned greater respect for himself and for his superiors and subordinates.

With the encouragement of his mentor and coach, Colonel L.T. "Babe" Godfrey, Bill directed his energy and toughness to athletics. He played baseball, football, and basketball, and also fought on the boxing team. He practiced teamwork and tenacity. As a senior, he led the basketball team to an undefeated season, and for two years running, he was a New Mexico Golden Gloves champion.

Bill was only five feet, six and three-quarter inches tall, but he had honed his body to be solid, muscular,

and tough. It struck Coach Godfrey that Bill was as indestructible as an Army vehicle and awarded him the nickname "Jeep," which was quickly adopted by students and instructors alike.

Throughout his life, Bill remained trim and strong. The toughness stayed with him, too, as did the lessons he learned from Coach Godfrey.

"He has been a magnificent mentor to me," said Bill, "and I have tried to follow his principles." Bill said his coach taught him, "When things are going bad, that's when to work three times as hard." Coach Godfrey also showed Bill what it means to compete on a team, to rely

Bill attended NMMI for four years; two years of high school and two years of junior college.

I'll never forget Coach Godfrey or the difference one person can make in turning around another person's life —

on others, and to win together. Unlike when he used to take over for his brother in a fight, Bill learned to let others bring their best to the contest, too. Bill never forgot his coach or the difference one person can make in turning around another person's life. For the next 45 years, Bill stayed in touch with Coach Godfrey and visited him twice a year to show his gratitude.

Bill made friends easily and enjoyed getting to know young cadets from all over the country. As he developed discipline, he learned how to discipline others, and he gradually became a leader. Bill was captain of "B" Troop his last year at NMMI. He took pride in reminding other cadets of NMMI's Honor Code, adopted in 1921: "A cadet will not lie, cheat or steal, nor tolerate those who do."

It wasn't that Bill had a spotless record of adherence to the code. One night, he placed a dummy in his bed and went out on a date, hoping that his absence would go undetected. No such luck.

Bill always remembered how the commandant of cadets, Colonel H. B. Saunders, Jr., handled the infraction. After making Bill wait in his private office for quite a while, Colonel Saunders came in and said, "Sit down, Jeep." Bill sat. "Jeep, you lied to me."

"Yes, sir, I did."

"I should throw you out of school."

"Oh, God. You can't do that, Colonel Saunders."

"Why can't I?"

"My dad would kill me. It would break his heart."

The colonel said, "Well, I'll call you back in about half an hour."

After another period of worrying, Bill returned to the commandant's office. "Jeep," he said, "I'm gonna give you a *second chance*. Remember that: a second chance." Giving others a second chance became one of Bill's guiding principles in life.

Bill stayed at NMMI for four years — two years of high school and two years of junior college. In the summers between school years, he worked as an oilfield roughneck and pipeliner. "That was really rough," Bill remembered. "We'd start out pipelining in the morning, and the boss would point to a spot on the horizon and say, 'That's where we're gonna be tonight.' "

Being an outdoor laborer added to Bill's wide range of job experiences. So did the NMMI requirement that he learn to ride a horse as part of the military school's cavalry training. Bill reflected on the time he spent at Fort Bliss, a US Army cavalry post on the Texas-New Mexico border. "After that, I made up my mind that I wanted to be a fighter pilot rather than having to rub down a horse after every ride," he said.

ABOVE | *The NMMI logo.* OPPOSITE | *No stranger to hard work and long days, Bill worked during the summers as an oilfield roughneck and pipeliner.*

CHAPTER FOUR

COURAGE, CHARACTER, AND GRATITUDE: A NAVY FIGHTER PILOT IN TWO WARS

People say to me that I am a real hero because I graduated from flight training two weeks after Pearl Harbor. Hero, my ass! I had no idea our nation would be at war. I entered flight training in 1941 and just wanted to fly in the Navy. I wanted to be a carrier-based fighter pilot.

~ Bill Daniels

When Bill graduated from New Mexico Military Institute in 1941, he immediately entered the US Navy's fighter pilot program. He was sent first to Los Alamitos Naval Air Station in California for flight and officer training. A telegram from Bill to his dad in Hobbs — sent just after Bill's 21st birthday — reveals a cocky young man not long past boyhood. "Just call me Ace," Bill transmitted. "Came through fine. Home about Wednesday. Broke till Monday and need about ten. Please loan."

Bill's training continued in Jacksonville and Miami, Florida. He graduated as a fighter pilot and ensign in December 1941, just two weeks after the Japanese attacked the US Navy base at Pearl Harbor, Hawaii,

---

OPPOSITE | *A young, handsome Bill in his Navy whites.* ABOVE | *Bill's military service during World War II was always a source of great pride.*

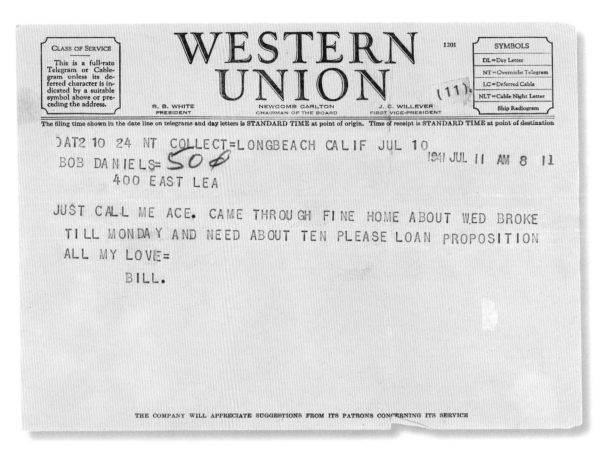

The filing time shown in the date line on telegrams and day letters is STANDARD TIME at point of origin. Time of receipt is STANDARD TIME at point of destination

DAT2 10 24 NT COLLECT=LONGBEACH CALIF JUL 10

BOB DANIELS= 50¢

1941 JUL 11 AM 8 11

400 EAST LEA

JUST CALL ME ACE. CAME THROUGH FINE HOME ABOUT WED BROKE
TILL MONDAY AND NEED ABOUT TEN PLEASE LOAN PROPOSITION
ALL MY LOVE=

BILL.

THE COMPANY WILL APPRECIATE SUGGESTIONS FROM ITS PATRONS CONCERNING ITS SERVICE

drawing the United States into World War II. Bill always downplayed this timing, pointing out that it was simply coincidence that he was freshly prepared to fly fighter planes just as his country went to war.

"People say to me that I am a real hero because I graduated from flight training two weeks after Pearl Harbor," Bill said. "Hero, my ass! I had no idea our nation would be at war. I entered flight training in 1941 and just wanted to fly in the Navy. I wanted to be a carrier-based fighter pilot." Whether it was luck or providence, Bill's new skills were invaluable to his country.

By February of 1942, Ensign Daniels was undergoing fighter squadron training in Norfolk, Virginia, and qualifying for carrier landings aboard the USS *Ranger*. Bill was thrilled with his pay of $187.50 a month. "I had never seen so much money," he said. "And the Navy always pays you in brand new bills, too."

As a carrier-based fighter pilot, Bill flew several different fighter planes during World War II, including the F4F Wildcat, F6F Hellcat, and F8F Bearcat (Bill's favorite). He served with distinction in Escort Fighting Squadron 26 attached to the aircraft carrier USS *Sangamon*. His combat missions supported the invasion of North Africa (to secure the Moroccan coast in the fight against Adolf Hitler) and many battles in the Pacific Theater. Bill spent almost a year as a land-based fighter pilot in the Solomon Islands, flying hundreds of missions to protect American soldiers and ships.

When Bill was assigned to a night-fighter squadron, he learned to navigate over open water with strict radio silence and to land on an aircraft carrier with no lights, all to avoid detection by the enemy. "It was a hell of a ride," Bill remembered.

Still young and a bit reckless, Bill once traded planes with his friend and fellow pilot Donal "Broe" Broesamle, just for a lark. Bill remembered the event in a letter he wrote years later to Broe:

The telegram that a cocky young Bill sent in 1941 shows he still needed a little help from his dad.

We both were based in Honolulu when I met you at a landing strip on the north part of the island. I met you in an F4U Corsair and you arrived in a P47. We gave each other a cockpit check out on the aircraft and proceeded to take off and circle the islands. When we got back, we got into our own airplanes. Looking back, I know we would have both been court-martialed, but what a fun experience. I can remember when I took off I thought, 'My God, I don't even know how to get the wheels up on this mother!' We both survived, and I have chuckled about this for years. Being young fighter pilots we felt we were bullet proof and half crazy. But that is what it took in those days for us to survive. We have both been damn lucky.

TOP | *In this photo taken on an aircraft carrier during World War II, Bill is pictured kneeling on the far right.* BOTTOM | *Bill in the cockpit.*

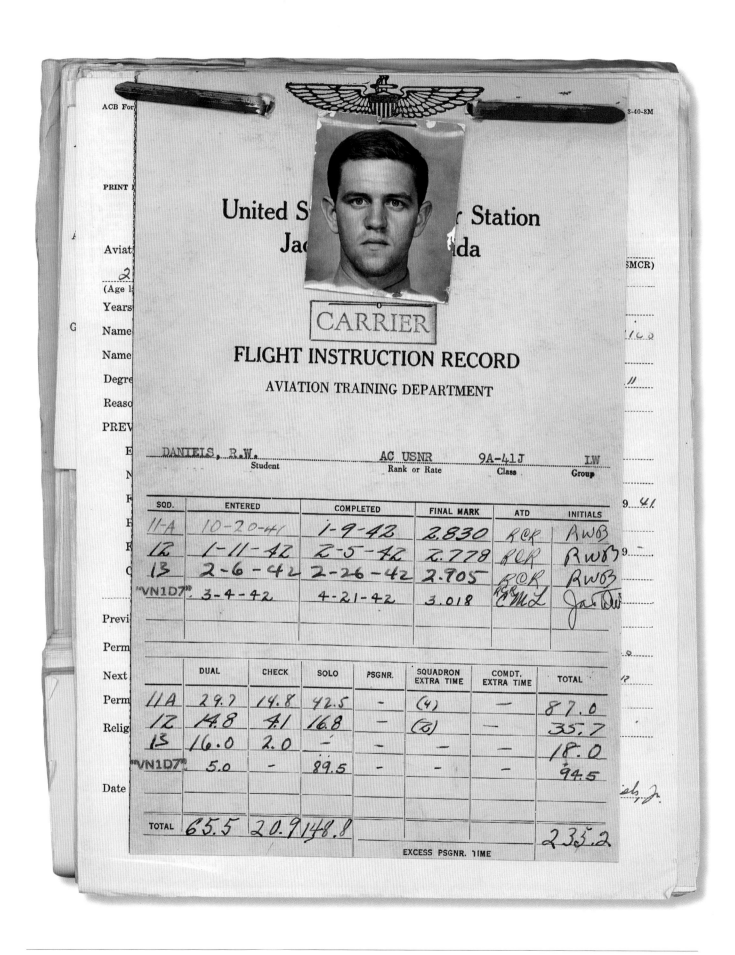

Bill's flight instruction record from the Naval Air Station in Jacksonville, Florida.

ABOVE | *As a carrier-based fighter pilot, Bill flew several different fighter planes during World War II, including the F4F Wildcat, F6F Hellcat, and his favorite, the F8F Bearcat.* INSET | *Bill's Naval aviator card.*

In 1943, Bill was sent to what he called "fighter director school" on St. Simons Island, Georgia, and then was assigned to the newly commissioned aircraft carrier USS *Intrepid*. Bill and his fellow fighter pilots strafed Japanese ships and island outposts to enable US Marines to capture the Marshall Islands (February 1944) and Allied Forces to win the Battle of Leyte Gulf (October 1944), which was considered to be the largest Naval battle of World War II.

There were several aircraft carriers in the fleet during this battle, and when one was hit and damaged, fighter pilots coming in to land were told to head to a different, undamaged carrier. When a carrier did not have room on the flight deck because of planes already parked there, the crew promptly shoved high-priced airplanes overboard to create room for incoming planes. Bill never forgot this expensive but necessary move to save lives.

He was on board the *Intrepid* on November 25, 1944, when it was hit by *kamikazes*, the infamous Japanese pilots who committed suicide by crashing their planes into enemy ships, causing great damage. "I was in the ready room, two decks below flight deck," Bill

The United States and its Allies fought a brutal air-sea-land campaign against the Japanese for possession of Guadalcanal. In this photo taken on the island, Bill is pictured second from left.

Bill was presented the Bronze Star for rescuing shipmates aboard the aircraft carrier USS Intrepid *after two Japanese kamikaze pilots dove their aircraft into the ship on November 25, 1944.*

(SEAL)

honorably discharged just about the time the Japanese were defeated.

"I really liked living the Navy life," Bill reflected later. But he was long haunted by the deaths of fellow pilots. "I went through one tough period during World War II when I saw so many of my squad mates and friends fail to return from missions or killed right before my eyes," Bill wrote decades later. "The chaplain used to tell us, 'Now, they are back with God,' and that was tough on me. I went through a couple of years after that when I was unhappy with our Lord. I felt those guys were taken. I think they should have been as lucky as I was to return home to their families . . . I have gotten over it, but I don't really understand it. I still have a problem with it."

To remind him of his good fortune, Bill hung a picture on his wall of one of the planes he flew during the war. "It reminded me how damn glad I was to get out of there alive," he said. "I was going to work hard, have a good time, and count my blessings every day that I was still walking around."

Back in Hobbs after the war, Bill went to work in his father's insurance business. His mother hoped he'd go to school and become a doctor, but Bill told her, "I don't want to wait another seven to nine years to start making some money."

When his brother, Jack, returned from his service on a Navy destroyer, he joined the insurance business, too. By this time, Bob Daniels was ill from heart problems and alcoholism, and the boys were a big help in holding the business together. They took it over entirely when their father died of a heart attack on June 1, 1948, shortly before his 55th birthday.

When Bill turned 30, he was still working with his brother, living in the small town of Hobbs, and going nowhere fast. "I wasn't doing what I wanted to do," he remembered.

Then he was called back to active duty as a Navy fighter pilot to serve in the Korean Conflict. *Nothing better than being a fighter pilot,* Bill remembered thinking. By August

remembered. "The ship was on fire, and one of my squad mates was trapped with his leg half blown off. I had to apply a tourniquet, cut off the rest of his leg, administer morphine, and carry him up two flights to the flight deck for help." Bill carried several other injured men to safety as the blaze was extinguished. For this heroic service, Bill was awarded the Bronze Star.

Bill Daniels spent all but five months of World War II on combat duty and served under well-known admirals Chester W. Nimitz and William Frederick "Bull" Halsey, Jr. On three occasions, the US Navy awarded Bill the Air Medal for his airmanship, courage, and devotion to duty during World War II. He returned to the United States in the spring of 1945, just as the Allies declared victory in Europe. He spent that summer ferrying fighter aircraft from Brooklyn to San Diego and was

Bill's aviator wings sit on top of one of Bill's early official Navy photographs.

1950, he was back on an aircraft carrier. Bill remembered the first evening he took off from the USS *Bairoko* and flew along the coast of South Korea. "I looked around and said to myself, 'What am I doin' way out here again?'"

Something pretty incredible, as it turned out. While serving in Korea, Bill was also assigned to the aircraft carrier USS *Boxer*. There he piloted the Grumman F9F-2 Panther, which helped lead the Navy's transition to jet-propelled aircraft.

Upon returning to the United States, Bill concluded his service at the Naval Air Station in Corpus Christi, Texas. He conducted flight instruction there for pilots learning to fly the Grumman Panther jet fighter. Among

them was a group of the Navy's best that would go on to serve as the Blue Angels flight demonstration team.

Bill's association with the Blue Angels was a source of deep pride for him, and he felt honored to have instructed some of the finest pilots in the world. It was a fitting final chapter of a distinguished and decorated military career.

In November 2005, the Sea-Air Operations Gallery at the Smithsonian Air and Space Museum in Washington, D.C., was dedicated in memory of Bill Daniels. The educational exhibit features an F4F Wildcat and displays replicas of Bill's World War II helmet and goggles as well as his Bronze Star and Air Medals.

In November 2005, the Sea-Air Operations Gallery at the Smithsonian Air and Space Museum in Washington, D.C., was dedicated in Bill's memory. The educational exhibit features a replica of the Grumman F4F Wildcat that Bill flew in World War II and displays replicas of Bill's helmet and goggles, as well as some of his medals.

CHAPTER FIVE

OPPORTUNITY, VISION, AND DRIVE: A PIONEER OF CABLE TELEVISION

If there is any reason for people to call me the 'Father of Cable Television,' I would think it would be because I was the first guy to recognize it as a hell of a potential business, and I brought the financial community in to really make it a business.

~ Bill Daniels

Bill in the mid-1960s.

Over the course of his life, Bill Daniels became well known as a visionary and innovator who continually sowed seeds of opportunity. "You never know when a sweet deal is going to walk in the door or who you're going to be talking to," Bill reflected in his later years.

His instincts about people and possibilities were what guided him.

Bill was a stickler for appearances, but he was also a keen observer of human behavior and could read people remarkably well. In the late 1940s — while Bill was working in his father's insurance business in Hobbs, New Mexico, before going to Korea — a man walked into the agency looking for someone to notarize several documents. Dressed like a laborer in khakis, the man was someone Bill thought just needed a break and a little

Bill stands in front of his insurance company offices in Casper, Wyoming.

help. Bill happily notarized every page for the man, a service that normally would have cost about $5. "But I said, 'No charge, sir. We're happy to have you in our city. Come back any time.' "

About three years later, the same gentleman walked into the insurance office in a three-piece suit. "By that time, he owned seven drilling rigs," said Bill. "He laid the insurance account on my lap and said, 'I want you to write the insurance on this.' " Over the next two years, that fellow brought more than $600,000 in insurance business into the Daniels Insurance Agency. When Bill asked him why he returned to the small agency for his business, he said, "I came in here three years ago, and you notarized some papers for me and you didn't charge me. You couldn't have been nicer and more polite." For Bill, this was a classic case of the adage he often repeated, "You never know who you're talking to."

The theme of "You never know . . . " would guide Bill for years to come and result in many surprising opportunities. He couldn't have anticipated the unique twists his career would take.

———————

After Bill's stint in Korea was over, he returned to Hobbs, fully expecting to work with his brother, Jack, in the insurance agency that bore the family name. But Jack had been running things on his own for two years while Bill was in Korea and didn't see a place for Bill in the family insurance business anymore. Jack bought his brother out for $5,000, and Bill was on his own.

He drove all over the Rocky Mountain area, looking for a place to open his own insurance business. He settled on Casper, Wyoming, population 25,000, where a new oil boom was underway. Within a short period of time, Bill built his business into one of the state's largest.

One day, during what would have been a routine trip from Hobbs to Casper, Bill stopped at Murphy's Bar on South Broadway in Denver for a beer and a corned-beef sandwich. A small black-and-white television was mounted over the bar showing *Wednesday Night Fights*, broadcast live from New York City.

It was the first time Bill had laid eyes on a television. His first thought was, "My God, what an invention this is!" For young people today who can't imagine life before the Internet and before television had hundreds of channels, it might be hard to fathom Bill's reaction. But prior to the 1950s, radio was the most advanced technology bringing news and entertainment into people's homes.

Americans watched movies in movie theaters and kept up with the news of World War II by watching black-and-white newsreels that rolled before the feature film. But the idea that a boxing match being fought at that moment on the East Coast could be watched on a little black-and-white screen in a Denver bar, well, that was like magic.

Bill remembered, "I couldn't get it out of my mind. How do you get that great invention to a small town that didn't have any TV stations?" Back in Casper, no one owned a television set, because no TV signal made it over the mountains. Individuals in a few other small cities — most notably in Oregon and Pennsylvania — had pioneered the use of cables that carried TV signals from larger cities, but their methods at the time were unreliable, expensive, and not widely understood.

Although he had no head for electronics or engineering, Bill found others who did, including brothers Richard and Gene Schneider, who had trained as engineers during the war. They worked on the technical challenges of bringing television broadcasts from Denver to Casper, while Bill persuaded local oilmen and bankers to back the project. It was not an easy feat. "It was tough raising money in those early days," Bill said. "Everyone thought I was nuts."

He was able to negotiate a deal with AT&T for help in transmitting the signal, and he persuaded local appliance stores to stock televisions for future customers. It was the beginning of a lifetime of dealmaking, collaboration, and raising capital.

On January 1, 1954 — college football bowl game day — the people of Casper, Wyoming, were able to tune their television sets to Denver's Channel 2, being broadcast 300 miles away. Within a year, 4,000 Casper homes were hooked up and paying a subscription fee of $7.50 a month. Bill's new venture was a success, and there was no turning back. "After about two years in the business, I knew we were going to have a wired nation one day," Bill said.

Following the success in Casper, Bill built cable systems in Rawlins, Wyoming, and Farmington, New Mexico, and he got to know other cable entrepreneurs through the new trade group he helped found, the National Community Television Association (NCTA). The organization was later renamed the National Cable & Telecommunications Association.

"If there is any reason for people to call me the 'Father of Cable Television,'" Bill reflected near the end of his career, "I would think it would be because I was the first guy to recognize it as a hell of a potential business, and I brought the financial community in to really make it a business."

After driving all over the Rocky Mountain area looking for a place to open his oil insurance business, Bill settled on these offices in Casper, Wyoming.

CHAPTER SIX

ETHICS, INTEGRITY, AND RELATIONSHIPS:
A BROKER OF FAIR DEALS

A person's integrity is the cornerstone of success in business and an indispensable part of personal relationships built on trust.

~ Bill Daniels

When asked by a reporter in 1994 what people who had done business with Bill Daniels would say about him, Bill replied, "I hope they would say I was reasonably intelligent; that I was a visionary and long-range thinker; that I was a true entrepreneur; that I was a man of great integrity, which I value highly; that I was highly ethical and handled myself properly; and that if I shook hands on a deal, it was just as good as a contract."

Those traits had certainly captured the attention of his colleagues some 40 years earlier. In 1956 — within two years of bringing the first television signal to Casper

ABOVE | *As Daniels & Associates grew, Bill devoted long hours to brokering deals for cable television systems.* OPPOSITE | *Bill stands proudly in front of the early offices of Daniels & Associates at 2930 East 3rd Avenue in Denver.*
Courtesy of Barco Library, The Cable Center

— Bill had earned enough respect to be elected the second president of the National Community Television Association (NCTA). Shortly after taking the reins, he began to tackle the industry's challenges head-on. A long fight between the established television networks and the fledgling cable companies — one that would continue for decades — was already brewing.

Battle lines were drawn. Broadcasters felt the cable industry was charging for services that they hadn't provided. Telephone companies didn't want the cable companies to use poles furnished (and paid for) by the telephone companies.

In response, Bill helped establish NCTA's lobbying office in Washington, D.C. "I can remember the early days

of cable TV when I would walk in the halls of both the House and Senate, and people who knew my profession would plead with me to break the monopoly of the three networks," said Bill.

Cable had raised the rancor of ABC, CBS, and NBC, as well as AT&T, local television stations, the Federal Communications Commission, and some local and state policymakers. Like the scrappy kid who became a Golden Gloves champion, Bill didn't back down. "My attitude at that time," Bill remembered, "was if all these people were busting their asses to stop our business from succeeding, we must have something. If we didn't, they could care less about us."

When the cable industry eventually prevailed — after

In the 1960s, Bill bought a Learjet so he could travel to business meetings faster than anyone else. His motto was, "I want to get there first."

what some described as a "big bloody battle in Congress" — Bill saw it as a victory for the consumer and a classic case of the free enterprise system at its best.

During his term as leader of the NCTA, Bill was approached by several fellow members who wanted to know how to buy or sell a cable system. With knowledge of just about every member's business activities, Bill found he could offer helpful, solid advice, but he didn't begin charging for that advice until his term as president was over. For Bill, it was a simple matter of ethics. He was building a reputation as a highly ethical businessman, and he fully realized the potential for an emerging business opportunity in brokering cable deals.

In 1958, Bill founded Daniels & Associates, the company that would anchor the rest of his career. The company's mission was to match buyers and sellers of cable television properties and to facilitate investment in the cable industry. He rented a one-room office in a downtown Denver bank building and began serving clients.

An early, significant deal came as a result of a chance meeting at a dinner in Rapid City, South Dakota, where Bill was a guest speaker. In his customary friendly way, Bill quickly introduced himself to the man sitting next to him and asked what he did for a living. The man introduced himself as Charles A. Sammons from Dallas and said he was in the life insurance business. Remembering the event years later, Bill commented, "I've been in that business, and I can tell you it's a tough business. If you can sell life insurance, you can sell anything."

The two men visited during the dinner and got along great. Not long after their conversation, Mr. Sammons wrote a letter to Bill, telling him he wanted to buy some of the cable systems they had discussed

"I didn't know who the hell he was," said Bill. "But I immediately called some friends in Dallas and said, 'Get me the book on C. A. Sammons.' And once I found out who he was, I couldn't get to Dallas soon enough." Bill found the systems, bought them on his new client's behalf,

> I'M PROUD THAT OUR SYSTEMS ARE PRAISED FOR THEIR QUALITY FACILITIES, EXCELLENT BUSINESS PRACTICES, INNOVATIVE PROGRAMMING, FIRST-CLASS CUSTOMER SERVICE, AND DEDICATED COMMUNITY INVOLVEMENT.

and managed them. The result was the creation of one of the first multi-system operators (MSOs) in the industry.

The chance encounter at a dinner brought Bill and his company more than $10 million over the next five years. "You never know who you're sitting next to," Bill reminded a group of business students many years later. But his genuine interest in other people wasn't just because he was on the alert for possible business opportunities. That was true. But more important, he had a sincere curiosity about people and what made them tick, and it showed. He had an uncanny ability to recall personal details about people long after he had met them.

Gayle Greer, who worked with Bill for many years in the cable industry, reflected on Bill's sincere interest in people. "I remember going to a cable meeting with Bill," she said. "It was at the City and County Building in Denver. A lot of people were gathered in the hallway, including what appeared to be janitors or laborers working in City Hall. Bill went over to them to say 'hello' or find out a little about them. I was so impressed because there we were, waiting to meet with the mayor, and Bill took the time to talk to people who really had nothing to do with what we were there for. It was just Bill being Bill."

The first Daniels & Associates building was located at 2930 East 3rd Avenue in Denver. These offices were later torn down, and the Daniels Communications Center offices were built at the same location.

With his legendary people skills and business acumen, before long Bill was brokering multimillion-dollar deals and raising capital for cable ventures across the country. In the process, he transformed bankers and Wall Street investors from skeptics into believers, but he always kept a firm grip on the elements of good business deals. He kept a sign on his desk that read, "Neither a scrooge nor a patsy be." He explained, "That means 'don't milk every deal for every dime you can; make a fair deal.' "

By the mid-1960s, Bill had bought a Learjet, so he could travel to business meetings faster than anyone else. "I wanted to get there *first*," he said, "and I did." Sometimes he flew the plane himself, but most often he used a pilot, so he could read and work during the flight.

He developed a demanding schedule, rising at 4:00 a.m. to read several newspapers, then working long days, seven days a week. At night, he made the most of the cocktail-party culture of the era. "I love work," he told one reporter. "I'm on vacation every hour of every day. I don't need to get away because there's so much diversion in my life."

Over the years, Bill owned and operated hundreds of cable television systems in virtually every state in the nation. His cable systems were praised for their quality facilities, excellent business practices, innovative programming, first-class customer service, and dedicated community involvement. Other companies in the cable industry were drawn to the opportunities Bill generated.

Bill with his assistant, Naida Fordyce, working in the early 1960s.

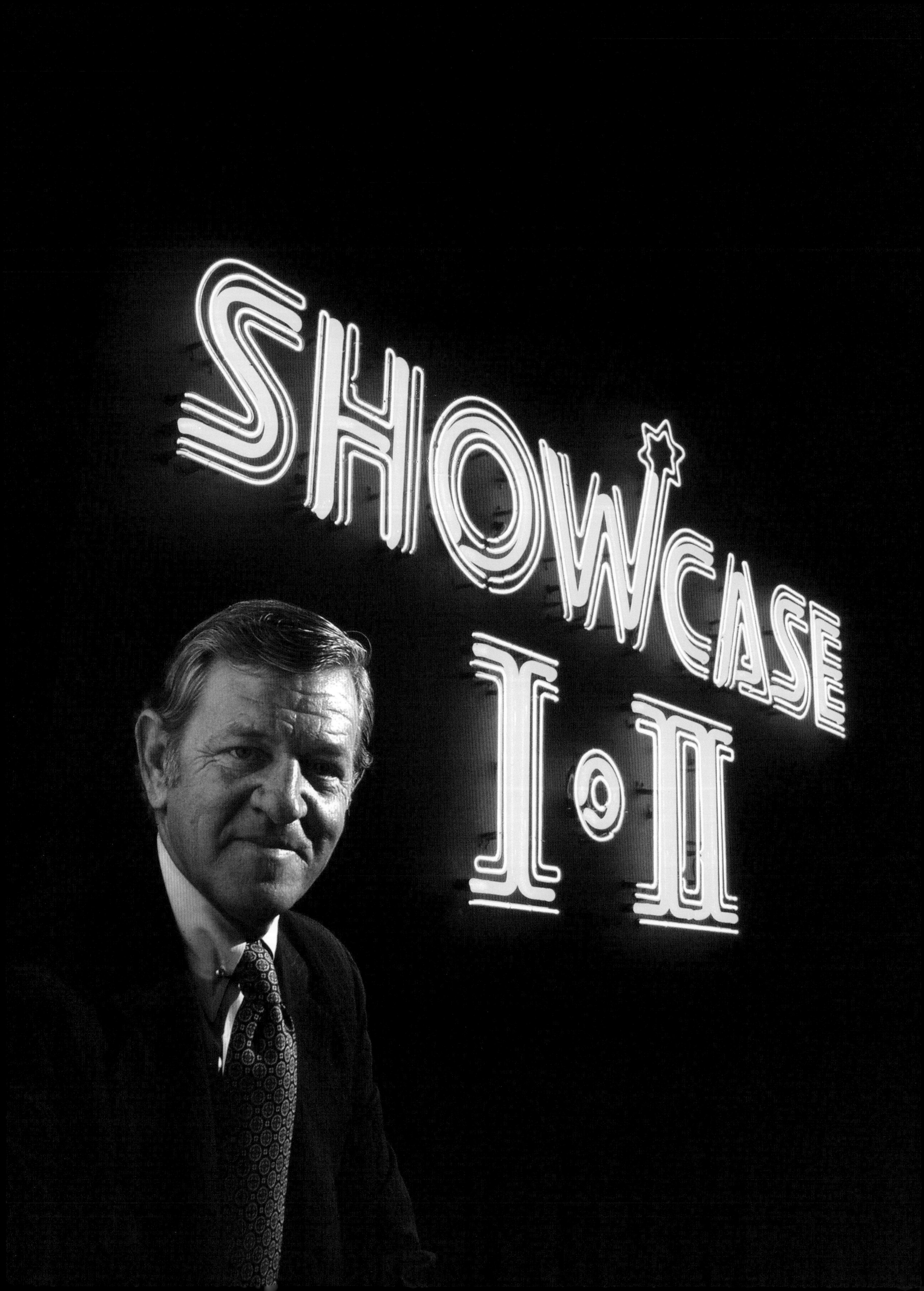
SHOWCASE
I · II

As a result, Denver became known as the "Cable Capital" of the United States.

Bill knew what he did well — and what he didn't. "Once the deal is put together, my history is I walk from it and let the good operations and administrative guys run the property," he explained in an article in *Cablevision Magazine*. "What made me feel that I was in the right business is that I can handle people so well. I knew every guy in the country who was in the cable business, visited every cable property, and traveled continually. I knew their families; they had confidence in me."

They had good reason to believe in Bill Daniels. Not only did he excel in his work, but he did it with the utmost integrity. As a publisher in the cable industry, once observed, "Every decision he ever made was based around what he thought was *right* as opposed to what he thought was *best* for him."

To everyone he encountered — from colleagues to MBA students to the children of his associates — Bill repeated his message of integrity. "A person's integrity is the cornerstone of success in business and an indispensable part of personal relationships built on trust," he said. "I have worked all of my life to maintain a reputation for honesty, fair dealing, and maintaining my integrity and my ethical outlook."

People loved Bill Daniels, and he loved people, but for much of his life he reserved his greatest passion and focus for his work. He'd arrive at work early and lay out a stack of index cards on his desk. Each one was carefully annotated with a task that he wanted to accomplish that day. After careful consideration, Bill methodically arranged each one of the cards in the order that he wanted to tackle the tasks inscribed upon them, put them into his pocket, and got to work.

He'd also do whatever was necessary to make a deal, no matter what the day or time. "I would leave town on Christmas day to do a deal," he told the *New York Times*. "I'm in love with my business."

His busy, high-profile career filled his life with friends and activity but was not conducive to deep, personal relationships or to a settled home life. "My business always came before my love affairs," he said.

Though Bill was married and divorced four times over the course of his life, he never blamed his spouses for his shortcomings as a husband. He spoke openly about his inability to maintain a happy marriage — a fact that he considered a major failure in his life. "I was more interested in my business, and I am ashamed of that," he said. "I have seen a lot of friends who built an empire and have a great family. I was unable to do that."

But he was also known to treat his ex-wives with dignity and generosity. When asked what his beliefs were about reincarnation, he chuckled and answered that if there were such a thing, he would want to come back as one of his ex-wives.

OPPOSITE | *In 1976, Bill launched Showcase I & II, early pay-TV channels offering movies, stage plays, nightclub performances, live entertainment, and sports programming. Delivered over his central Texas cable systems, these channels were innovative because they allowed customers to choose the specific programming options they would like to receive.* Courtesy of Barco Library, The Cable Center

CHAPTER SEVEN

TEAMWORK, TRUST, AND LOYALTY: A GENEROUS LEADER AND MENTOR

You will find this company one of the easiest ones to work for, and I am tolerant of many faults, as I have many, but I will not tolerate sloppiness, untidiness, and unkempt areas.

~ Bill Daniels

COURTESY OF BARCO LIBRARY, THE CABLE CENTER

As Daniels & Associates grew, Bill needed a capable right-hand man. He found that person in John Saeman, who joined the company in 1965. John, a Marine, was working at Subscription Television, Inc. in California. When he met Bill Daniels at a cable convention, they were mutually impressed.

After nearly 20 years of working together, John had glowing remarks about Bill. "The way I measure success

---

John Saeman (at right) was Bill's friend and capable right-hand man during the growth of Daniels & Associates.

"This fall, nothing sells basic like CNN."

"This year's election — the way Cable News Network is covering it — is one of the best things that ever happened to make people aware of cable.

"CNN is making it clear to everyone that Basic Cable offers news with a depth and convenience that ordinary TV can't match.

"It's a perfect time to sell Basic, and CNN is giving us the perfect tools to do it. They're giving us a complete election promotion kit that includes newspaper and guide ads, bill stuffers, radio spots, printed outdoor boards, and videotaped TV commercials.

"Best of all, CNN pays for it — 100% reimbursement up to 8¢ a subscriber.

"All you have to do is get out your CNN promotion package and run the advertising. There's never been a better time to promote the cable difference."

For details or an additional promotion kit, call your Turner Representative at (404) 827-2250.

Bill Daniels, Chairman
Daniels & Associates

CNN
CABLE NEWS NETWORK

is not only his business accomplishments, but what kind of human being he is," said John. "There are few human beings that I think are any better than Bill. He's just a very warm, giving individual."

Bill's philosophy of management was focused on courtesy and mutual respect. "I've always told people they don't work for me," said Bill, "they work *with* me." And the people who worked with him were called associates, not employees.

About his role as head of a large company, Bill explained, "People want more than a paycheck for their efforts; they want to know you care about them. They want you to listen to their ideas, to be open to their suggestions, and to provide them with a good office environment. There's a common misconception in the workplace: People always feel they have to please the

boss. If a company is to be truly successful, it has to be the other way around."

When Tom Marinkovich joined the Daniels & Associates team in 1980, he found Bill to be the most trusting person he had ever known. "He would lead by example, but he trusted his executives to take over and get it done," said Tom. "He had a great ability to focus on the person he was talking to, and he made you feel like you were the only one in the room."

Working with his capable team, Bill achieved results in the cable industry that were unparalleled. In 1968, he formed American Television & Communications Corporation (ATC). Two years later, he had the pleasure of writing to a friend who had invested $33,743 in ATC to report the stock was now worth $99,184. In usual Daniels style, he completed the letter by saying, "In all

An early advertisement promoting Cable News Network. Bill helped raise $10 million so Ted Turner could launch CNN in 1980.

largest individual shareholder in Turner Broadcasting System (TBS). Bill's stake in TBS (which owned CNN) was second only to Ted's. Bill served on the CNN board of directors, and when Turner threw the switch to turn on the world's first 24-hour news channel, Bill stood right by his side. Bill was also an early investor in mobile communications and cellular systems.

In 1985, Bill partnered with Jerry Buss, owner of the Los Angeles Lakers, and launched Prime Ticket Network to broadcast Lakers basketball and L.A. Kings hockey games as well as other regional sports. As part of the deal, Bill became a five percent owner of the famed Lakers team. Bill's go-to guy for putting together the Prime Ticket agreement was Tony Acone, who became president of Prime Ticket and managed the operations.

"Bill handed me an envelope — some piece of mail he had received — with notes that he had written on the back," Tony remembered. "What he had asked me to do was to investigate the feasibility of putting together a regional sports network in Southern California. It was a new challenge, and we did it. Prime Ticket was the flagship of what became Prime Sports Network."

The merger of Prime Ticket and Home Sports Entertainment in 1988 gave Bill control of the nation's largest regional sports network. It served 4.5 million subscribers in Southern California, Arizona, Nevada, and Hawaii. He sold his interest in the network in 1994 to Tele-Communications, Inc. (TCI) and shared millions

sincerity, to hell with the stock, to hell with what we have made. The main thing is what a joy it has been for me to know you." By the late 1980s, ATC had become the nation's second-largest cable system and was owned by Time Inc.

Another close friend of Bill's was Ted Turner, who shared Bill's belief in the value of an all-news network. In what would mark another industry milestone, Bill helped raise $10 million so Ted could launch the Cable News Network (CNN) in 1980. Through a series of transactions, Bill would ultimately become the second-

With Bill at a launch party for the Prime Sports Network in 1988 was Olympic gold medalist Florence Griffith "Flo Jo" Joyner.

THERE'S A COMMON MISCONCEPTION
IN THE WORKPLACE:

PEOPLE ALWAYS FEEL THEY
HAVE TO PLEASE THE BOSS—

IF A COMPANY IS TO BE TRULY
SUCCESSFUL, IT HAS TO BE THE
OTHER WAY AROUND.

of dollars in proceeds with his associates at Prime Ticket to reward them for a job well done.

An earlier windfall for his associates came in 1988 when Bill merged 24 of his cable systems with United Artists Communications (UA). The sale netted $190 million for Daniels & Associates. Bill's personal share was almost $100 million, and everyone who worked at Daniels & Associates got a bonus.

"I've tried to share throughout my career," said Bill. "My philosophy has been simple. Since I've never had retirement programs, my theory is to try and put the money in the hands of individuals when they're at a young-enough age, rather than wait until they're 65 and too old to enjoy it."

Another of Bill's philosophies was to expect and demand *the best* in absolutely everything he touched. "There is only one way to do things, and that is first class. It pays off in the long run," said Bill.

When the new Denver headquarters of Daniels & Associates opened in 1982 at 3rd and Milwaukee in the heart of Cherry Creek, they were just that: first class. The

building cost $8.6 million and included a gym, sauna, racquetball court, high-tech conference room, and colorful, modern furnishings. Crystal and china used in the company's dining room were inscribed with the company name. Chiseled on a wall in the lobby was one of Bill's mottos, "The best is good enough for me."

"The best" was also what he expected from his associates in every possible way. One area he particularly stressed was the importance of appearances. Whether in a perfectly tailored suit and tie or in casual summer party clothes, Bill was known to be the finest dresser in the room. To Bill, how people dressed was a reflection of how much respect they had for others. Though his associates might not be able to buy from the same high-end clothing stores that Bill did, he advised them to "dress properly within your budget, and keep your shoes shined."

He also demanded that offices and desks stay tidy and well organized. "I cannot express to you how important it is to have a well-organized, neat-looking operation in every nook and cranny," he said. "Throughout my business career, primarily because of my military school training and my US Navy exposure, I have been a stickler for neatness and well-organized desks, including the mechanical rooms and the basement."

If his expectations for a neat and well-organized work area weren't met, the consequences were clear. "I have spent more money per square foot on each employee than any business or building owner in the state of Colorado, obviously to make working conditions pleasant, comfortable, and above all to establish a sense of pride," he wrote in a memo to his associates. "I feel so strongly about this that if you feel you cannot do this or you do not have the same pride in this building that I do, perhaps you should rethink your commitment to this company to see if it is the right fit for you."

Bill was also known to conduct surprise inspections of his company facilities, which could cause quite a scramble if he showed up unexpectedly.

Always on the cutting edge of technology, Bill sits at the head of the table in the executive conference room at the Daniels Communications Center in this 1983 photo. Individual televisions rise when needed for each person seated at the table.

TOP | *Nighttime view of the Daniels Communications Center.* BOTTOM | *Bill works in his offices at the Daniels Communications Center, surrounded by his memorabilia.*

Best boss?

Cable mogul Bill Daniels drives hard bargain with a soft touch

By MICHAEL ROMANO
Rocky Mountain News Staff Writer

BILL DANIELS, a visionary credited with creating America's modern cable-television industry, still rankles when associates fail to clean their desks around quitting time.

At 68, he remains utterly demanding and absolutely precise, a by-the-numbers boss whose work ethic is carved across the granite wall in the lobby of a Cherry Creek office building that bears his name: "The best is good enough for me."

Once, several years ago, this captain of commerce, this jet-setting entrepeneur whose net worth exceeds $50 million, spent the better part of an afternoon anguishing over the placement and height of the corporate flag that was to fly outside one of his headquarters buildings.

"Demanding? Bill expects you to *jump*," says Stewart Schley, who worked as director of corporate communications for Daniels & Associates before the cable czar sold part of his far-flung empire earlier this year to United Artists Communications Inc.

Adds another former associate, Erika Schafer, who worked with Daniels for 14 years: "Bill doesn't take no for an answer. He's not interested in knowing why a job can't be done. You just do it. And *now*."

Daniels disagrees, but only to a point: "I want it done *yesterday!*" he declares. "I'm impatient. It's a fault of mine. But they all get the message — I am impatient."

Yet Daniels instills a fervent loyalty among his network of "associates" (no one who works for Daniels is regarded simply as an employee).

Their cult-like devotion rests on the characteristic most uniformly ascribed to Daniels, a chain-smoking World II fighter-pilot who maintains his military demeanor. Friends and associates invariably focus on his sincerity and compassion, the caring concern that sustains the feeling of "family" within a corporate community he created three decades ago.

"You talk to Bill, and you're the only person in the world," marvels Jackie O'Brien, who has worked with Daniels for almost 13 years. "He'll remember everything you've told him — names of children, grandchildren — *everything*.

"He's not just a boss, not just a casual friend. Bill Daniels cares about people. Sure, he has his faults. But we overlook them, because the good outweighs the bad."

Like several other associates, Bob Russo, a senior vice president who has served on the right hand of Daniels since 1981, speaks of the chairman of the board with a the kind of wonderment and awe that approaches reverence.

"You sense that you're a member of his family," said Russo, who, as the company's top marketing executive, is paid to promote the distinctive aura of his well-known and somewhat eccentric boss. "You feel about him the way you would a father."

Of course, the tight familial bond is cemented by a legendary generosity. Daniels, a Greeley native, believes in sharing his wealth with those who helped him earn it. He has distributed millions and millions of dollars in bonuses to dozens of his associates.

Concerned about the health and welfare of his associates, Daniels included a weight room, saunas and a racquetball court in the basement of his former Cherry Creek headquarters, an $8.6 million building that opened in 1981 and now is named One Bill Daniels Centre.

HE ALSO routinely rewards his associates with "equity" shares in several of his companies — an extremely lucrative perquisite that serves as of an immediate retirement bonus.

"Benevolent? Baloney!" declares Daniels over a private lunch prepared by his personal chef in the company's new offices on Cherry Creek South Drive. "If people feel they're part of a company, if they feel they've got part of the action, don't you think they produce more?

"Business is people. And the people are the company. This company is not me. It's the people who work here."

Daniels began his Denver-based business in 1958 with one employee, a secretary. Since then, he has parlayed intuition and business moxie into one of the most widely regarded cable operations and investment-brokerage firms in the world, playing a part in the development of seven of the 10 largest cable networks in the United States.

In the late 1970s, Daniels raised $10 million to help Ted Turner launch Cable News Network, a then-novel idea that nearly everyone but Daniels and Turner expected to fail miserably.

Over the past three years, Daniels & Associates has delivered almost 50% of all cable mergers and acquisitions closed by a cable-brokerage firm. In 1987, the firm brokered 36 transactions worth $1.1 billion.

Daniels also has earned a handful of nicknames, most of them flattering. Among them: "Captain Video," a tag attributed to *Forbes* magazine. In a 1983 profile in the Sunday *New York Times*, Daniels was characterized as "the cable industry's No. 1 dealmaker," the father of modern cable television. CBS' *60 Minutes* has featured Daniels three times.

A consummate salesman, Daniels is fond of claiming that he would unhesitatingly leave home and family on Christmas Day to close a deal — one reason, perhaps, that the compact, ruddy-faced Daniels has been married and divorced four times.

"Dumbest SOB about women I've ever met," says Robert E. Lee, a Daniels vice president who has known the boss for 28 years. "He likes to have a good-looking women on his arm."

The peripatetic Daniels globe-hops from the cockpit of a Lear jet, enjoys the company of attractive younger women and lives in a palatial, 24,000-square foot Denver mansion that boasts 109 televisions and more than 100 telephones. On Shangri-La Drive, the home — used frequently by an assortment of charitable groups at no charge — has been named Cableland.

Former owner of the Utah Stars of the American Basketball Association and the Los Angeles Express of the World Football League, the sports-oriented Daniels holds an interest in the World Champion Los Angeles Lakers and counts star guard Earvin "Magic" Johnson among his friends.

Sports and politics represent Daniels' only

FRANK KIMMEL/Rocky Mountain News

> ❝ Benevolent? Baloney! If people feel they're part of a company, if they feel they've got part of the action, don't you think they produce more? Business is people. And the people are the company. This company is not me. It's the people who work here. ❞
>
> **Bill Daniels**

financial failures. He lost a hard-fought battle for the Republican gubernatorial nomination in 1974 and poured millions of dollars down the dual financial drains that were the A.B.A. and the W.F.L.

MY WEAKNESS is that a salesman is the biggest sucker in the world for another salesman," says Daniels, whose office walls are decorated with autographed portraits of presidents Kennedy, Johnson, Carter, Ford, Nixon and Reagan. (A huge portrait-poster of super model Christie Brinkley adorns one wall in his office bathroom).

For a highly visible, politically active and enormously wealthy man, Daniels apparently has made no enemies — at least not the public sort. Indeed, few negatives have ever been tied to Daniels in the many newspaper

and magazine profiles that have appeared over the years.

"You'd think that, simply by virtue of being around 30 years in business, that Bill would have some enemies," said Tim David, a Daniels & Associate senior vice president in charge of investment banking and brokerage services for the eastern U.S. "I really don't think he has any — except those who might be envious of his success."

Often outspoken and blustery, Daniels can be surprisingly self-effacing, tempering the irritating elements of his strong-willed personality with a private, philanthropic side that has earned him renown as one of Denver's "softest touches" for those in need.

"I thank God that somebody like him has been able to make a lot of money — because he's helped so many people with it," says Lee, noting the many charitable works asso-

See DANIELS, page 84

ABOVE | *A 1988 newspaper article describes Bill's demanding work ethic and generous reward programs at Daniels & Associates.*
OPPOSITE | *Bill was legendary as the driving force behind the expansion of cable television in America.*   PHOTO BY NICHOLAS DeSCIOSE

Associates at one of Bill's cable systems in California remembered the day Bill was on his way for a visit, and they realized the goldfish pond was overgrown with algae. In the last 20 minutes before Bill arrived, they removed the fish, emptied the water, took the pond apart, and placed a plant from someone's office onto the remaining concrete podium.

Despite their last-ditch efforts, the employees later received a scathing letter from Bill. After admonishing them for the conditions of the offices and other facilities, Bill announced that a Marine would be joining the company as an "enforcer." The letter went on to say, "You will find this company one of the easiest ones to work for, and I am tolerant of many faults, as I have many, but I will not tolerate sloppiness, untidiness, and unkempt areas." With tongue in cheek, he concluded the letter, "The good news is I write a letter like this about every five years. The bad news is you never know when I'm coming to town."

During a visit to his cable operations in Greeley, Colorado, Bill conducted another surprise inspection of the company's repair trucks parked in the yard. Back inside the office, he called a meeting of all the associates. For several minutes, he lectured them on the importance of keeping the trucks clean, and strongly expressed his dismay that so many trucks were filthy. Then he asked, "Who drives truck number five?" The driver warily raised his hand. Bill passed the man a $100 bill from his pocket and said, "I just want you to know I appreciate people who keep my equipment clean." The company manager never had to tell anyone to clean his truck again.

As a veteran entrepreneur and businessman, Bill grew naturally into the role of mentor. Home Box Office (HBO) founder Chuck Dolan observed in 1983, "When you talk with him, it's like speaking with your career counselor, 'What's your next move? What are you planning? How are you progressing?'"

Bill's generosity and care for his team generated a sense of loyalty and commitment that contributed to his company's success. "I think people would have died for Bill Daniels," said one associate.

However, they weren't about to let him die for them. After years of social drinking evolved into a serious problem with alcohol, Bill finally had to face his demons. Stress, rejection, work pressures, relationship problems, and restlessness were all issues that he confronted. Many times he turned to the bottle for fleeting comfort. The turning point came in 1985 when Bill disappeared for several days on a bender that ended in a hotel room in Scottsdale, Arizona.

Bill rarely went more than a day without talking to his associates. "All of a sudden, it went quiet," said John Saeman. "And we didn't hear from Bill for two or three days." John and others began calling friends, visiting Bill's typical haunts, looking for his car at airports, and calling hotels where he stayed frequently. No one had seen Bill.

Almost at the point of calling law enforcement officials to send out an all-points bulletin, John got a call from Bill's secretary, who announced she had heard from Bill and that he sounded bad.

Bill's brother, Jack — as well as John and other close colleagues — went to Bill's hotel room and found Bill drunk and disheveled. The resulting intervention led to rehab at the Betty Ford Center in Rancho Mirage, California. It was a major turning point for Bill Daniels.

When Bill emerged from the Betty Ford Center six weeks later, he was a changed man. Not only did he remain sober, but he also turned even this personally painful and potentially humiliating experience into a lesson for others. He talked openly about his battle with alcoholism, encouraged (and paid for) others to seek treatment, and even served on the board of the Betty Ford Center. For years, his letters and lectures often included an announcement of how many months or years he had gone without a drink.

The offices of Daniels & Associates, located in Denver at 3200 Cherry Creek South Drive, became known as RBC Daniels in 2007.

CHAPTER EIGHT

PATRIOTISM, POLITICS, AND FREE ENTERPRISE: A BUSINESSMAN IN POLITICS

I fought in two wars not only to save the freedom of our great nation but also to preserve the free enterprise system.

~ Bill Daniels

Bill Daniels loved America. One of his favorite quotes was by Winston Churchill, a man Bill greatly admired. "It has been said that democracy is the worst form of government," said Churchill, "except for all those other forms that have been tried from time to time." Believing that the right to vote was not just a right but an obligation, Bill often reminded his associates to vote. He also believed that politics was nothing more than "participation in government."

Bill raised untold sums for political candidates, held various positions in the Republican Party, and was elected as Republican National Committeeman in 1972.

"There were many things about government that disturbed me," Bill told his fellow Republicans

Bill during his 1974 campaign for governor of Colorado.

He lost the primary — after spending more than $400,000 of his own money — but he believed he had done his duty to emphasize the need for better ethics in state leadership. "Looking back on it," he said a decade later, "it's a blessing in disguise that I wasn't elected, because I would have lost four, possibly eight, years in my business career, which would have put me way behind. I probably never would have caught up."

Others certainly wished for many reasons that Bill had won the election. One reason was he would have brought honorable, upstanding traits to elected office. "Bill knew the importance of politics in providing a service and better quality of life for people, which was his ultimate goal," said Bill's longtime Republican colleague Jim Nicholson. "He was a role model for people, showing that you could be in politics and be a straightforward, honest person. You don't have to be small and gossipy. He showed how to be a bigger person in politics. That's what Bill was in politics, and that's what he was in life."

when explaining his decision to run for governor of Colorado in the 1974 election. "When dishonesty, conflicts of interest, the 'buddy-buddy system,' waste, and mismanagement cropped up, it was always brushed off by a comment of 'that's just politics.' I asked myself, 'Why should politics have a different set of values and ethics than any other part of our lives?'"

Bill campaigned in every county in the state and met wonderful people everywhere he went. It was important to him to set an example to other business leaders, and he encouraged many of them to consider elected office. "I have always felt we should have more businessmen in government," Bill said.

bill daniels

THE 8TH WONDER OF THE WORLD IS THE FREE ENTERPRISE SYSTEM...

AND THE 9TH WONDER OF THE WORLD IS SO FEW PEOPLE UNDERSTAND IT.

Campaign materials when Bill ran for Republican National Committeeman in 1972.

Bill DANIELS GOVERNOR ★

WHERE BILL DANIELS STANDS:

GOVERNMENT –– "The state of Colorado is our biggest business. Isn't it time it's headed by a business administrator, instead of by bureaucrats? Big government adds to the inflationary problems of the elderly and those on fixed incomes. As a businessman, I believe there are four basic ingredients which must be included in all decisions: Integrity, Compassion, Judgment and Common Sense. Those are the foundation of my campaign."

WELFARE –– "Let's eliminate the greedy and help the needy! Those who truly need assistance too often aren't getting it because of the frauds and cheats in the system. El Paso County has shown us the way to save at least $10 million a year on welfare payments -- and still provide better aid for those who need it. The State of Colorado, by contrast, continues to flounder around."

LAND USE –– "As a native Coloradoan, I'm determined to keep our state the greatest in the nation. We need long-range planning for effective action, not scattershot reaction to emergencies. We can't suppress workable growth in Colorado or we will stagnate. As governor, I would push hard for incentive programs that would channel small, clean, industries into our deprived counties, helping them economically and keeping the young at home by offering more jobs."

DEATH PENALTY –– "We must restore it. Nobody claims it will stop all capital crime. Still, the capital crime rate rises. So, I think it's time we started worrying more about the victim than the criminal. And that does not just go for capital crimes, either. Let's get tough!"

PENAL REFORM –– "One of the most neglected problems today. I've worked with parolees and prison inmates for a decade now and I know we're not providing the incentives we should to make these men viable human beings once they're on the outside again. Here's an area where businessmen can be a real help, with the right leadership."

EDUCATION –– "Forced busing is wrecking our opportunity for quality education. It's unfair, stupid and expensive. Why not spend the money instead to improve educational facilities of every child in Colorado? Forced busing is an encroachment on every man's Constitutional rights. And, as governor, I would work hard for a Constitutional amendment to get rid of this inexcusable situation. Now!"

POLITICAL ABUSES –– "Election to public office is a sacred trust. I've always run my life and my businesses in a manner of which I'm proud. I would conduct a public office the same way. All of my financial holdings will always be a matter of record."

"Serving as your Governor would be a major challenge. My life has been built on meeting challenges successfully."

Bill Daniels

What's Bill Daniels All About?

OPPOSITE | *Bill speaks to the media during his concession speech after losing the Republican primary for governor.* ABOVE | *Bill's campaign materials during his 1974 unsuccessful bid for governor of Colorado.*

For Bill, democracy and free enterprise were inseparable partners, working together for prosperity. To one US Congressman, he wrote, "I fought in two wars not only to save the freedom of our great nation but also to preserve the free enterprise system."

He believed the cable industry was an example of "the free enterprise system at its best," not only because it required risk takers to grow a new business out of a technology that never existed before but also because it created a large number of jobs for the US economy. To prove his assertion, Bill commissioned a study in 1990 called "Cable Cares" that found the cable industry was responsible for one percent of US job growth in the previous four years. The report estimated that the industry accounted for 561,000 jobs, and generated income of $18.2 billion.

"The eighth wonder of the world is the free enterprise system," Bill often said. "And the ninth wonder of the world is so few people understand it." His dream of helping people understand "it" resulted in his founding of the Young Americans Bank in 1987 to teach children early how to prosper in the free enterprise system.

This one-of-a-kind bank for kids is a real, state-chartered, FDIC-insured bank offering savings and checking accounts, personal and business loans, credit cards (with a low credit limit), and other banking services to people under age 22. Demand was high for such an institution. Nearly 2,000 accounts were opened in the bank's first three weeks. As Young Americans Bank grew, its programs expanded and eventually became a cornerstone of financial literacy education in area schools.

The success of the bank was a major source of pride for Bill. "I'm very proud of Young Americans Bank," he said during his acceptance speech for the Cable Television Hall of Fame in 1998. "It was a day most people said would never come. 'A bank for kids? Never.' That's what they said about *cable*."

TOP | *Though Bill was a staunch Republican, he was a friend to many presidents.* TOP RIGHT | *In 1988, Bill welcomed George H.W. Bush to his Denver residence for a Republican fundraising event that raised more than $300,000 for Bush's presidential campaign.*

CHAPTER NINE

WINNING, LOSING, AND PLAYING FAIR: AN INVESTOR IN SPORTS

It's all fun . . . if you can afford it.

~ Bill Daniels

O n June 21, 1988, Bill Daniels was watching the seventh game of the National Basketball Association championship series between the Los Angeles Lakers and the Detroit Pistons. As part owner of the Lakers (who were gunning for their second consecutive championship), Bill was dreaming of a win like everyone else. Late in the fourth quarter, the Lakers were up by 15 points, but the Pistons fought back. With just six seconds to go, the Pistons had narrowed the Lakers' lead to one point.

A wide variety of sports captured Bill's interest, but he lost so much money with his sports investments that he called them "charities."

Jerry Buss and Bill, co-owners of the Los Angeles Lakers, with Lakers star Magic Johnson.

Denver Officially Joins New International Boxing League

Denver has officially become a member of the new International Boxing League (IBL) and will immediately start putting together a squad of amateurs for competition starting in November.

This was announced Monday by Bill Daniels, holder of the franchise, and Vince Boryla, president of the Denver Boxing Club.

The team will be known as the Denver Rocks and will be in the Western Division of the IBL with St. Louis, Chicago and Milwaukee. The Eastern Division consists of New York City, Baltimore-Washington, Louisville and Miami.

The IBL, organized by Jack Drees, prominent radio and television personality, will operate on an amateur basis until such time that it grows in stature of the professional level.

The IBL teams will be sanctioned by the Amateur Athletic Union and operate under AAU rules as well as regulations of boxing commissions of the various cities and states.

Boryla said regional amateur boxers will compete for places on the Denver Rocks team in seven weight classes —bantamweight, featherweight, lightweight, welterweight, middleweight, light heavyweight and heavy-

Daniels   **Boryla**

programs in establishing the Denver Rocks.

"This inter-city boxing competition has been under study for two years and is now ready to get off the ground," Daniels said. "We have held many meetings and feel we have the answers to problems besetting the boxing game."

It was pointed out that the franchises are held by owners who can afford to meet all commitments for a successful operation of a program of such scope.

"We promise to provide the latest in modern training facilities, equipment and team handlers," Boryla said. "There are still a few details to be worked out concerning a first class gym but we will have one in the near future."

Boryla also said that popular prices of $3.50, $2.50 and $1.50 would prevail for the five home shows scheduled this fall and winter. The Denver team will

meet the three other Western Division teams on a home-and-home basis and would battle two Eastern Division teams here and away.

"The five shows here will be spaced about a month apart with road matches scheduled in the interim." Boryla explained, "Our colors will be red and white."

"The purpose of this program is to give a year-around athletic opportunity, fully supervised nad professionally coached, to a vast number of boys who enjoy individual sports competition such as boxing," Daniels explained.

Boryla added, "Competition for team berths will be a continuing thing and we intend to start the best fighters of the region in each weight class on every program."

He invited interested regional amateur boxers to contact the Denver Rocks at the team's office, 285 Milwaukee St. The telephone number is 321-1606.

Mayor Bill McNichols was present at the luncheon announcing the program and welcomed the IBL to Denver. Also in attendance was Police Chief George Seaton, members of the Colorado Athletic Commission, Eddie Bohn, Frederick Dickerson and Fritz Brennecke, and Pete Seipel and Russell Lyons

The tension was nearly too much for Bill. He sought divine intervention. "I closed my eyes and told the Lord that if the Lakers could win this ballgame, I would contribute $10,000 to Father Woody's food line," Bill remembered later. A last-second layup on a full-court pass from the famous Magic Johnson won the game for the Lakers, and the fans went wild.

Two days later, Bill sent a letter and check to Monsignor C. B. Woodrich, the priest of Denver's Holy Ghost Catholic Church. "Father Woody," as he was better known, was a beloved pastor who had become known as Denver's Patron Saint of the Poor.

"We won the game," Bill told Father Woody, "and the way I got it figured, if I don't live up to my promise to the Lord, He ain't gonna listen next time I have a problem."

Although Bill's investments in professional sports rarely had such a direct tie to charitable donations, he lost so much money with his sports enterprises that he called them "charities." But he enjoyed investing in athletes and teams so much that he kept doing it for decades.

Bill's lifelong passion for sports was perhaps most evident in his many boxing-related ventures.

It all started with boxing, which had been Bill's favorite sport since his boxing days at New Mexico Military Institute (NMMI). In the 1960s, he organized the Denver Boxing Club for amateurs and financed an adult boxing team, the Denver Rocks.

Then he met Ron Lyle, a boxer in the Colorado State Penitentiary. When the Young Presidents' Organization encouraged its members to do something about the nation's penal system, Bill took the suggestion seriously and started visiting area prisons. He grew close to some of the inmates, including Lyle, who was in prison for second-degree murder and had turned his life around through boxing.

After Lyle was paroled in 1969, he joined a boxing gym in Denver, and Bill sponsored him, along with several other professional boxers. "We're equal partners," Bill told reporters about his arrangements with these men. "They supply the talent and ability, and I supply their salaries, guidance, and other expenses. If there's anything left over, we split it evenly."

A huge milestone of Bill's boxing enterprise was Lyle's match on May 16, 1975 against heavyweight champion Muhammad Ali. It was a close fight and at times an upset seemed imminent. But Lyle lost in the 11th round.

Soon after, Lyle walked away from both his contract and his relationship with Bill Daniels. Though Bill lost $300,000 supporting Lyle's career, his disappointment with Lyle was about much more than money. "I was crushed," said Bill. "I will never figure out why he wanted to break up our arrangement. It was like being sued by your brother."

By that time, Bill had also lost money as owner of the American Basketball Association's Utah Stars. Bill had believed so much in the ABA's future that he served as league commissioner from 1971 to 1973. But no amount of leadership or investment could save his team and the league itself. Bill was heartbroken when the Utah Stars folded in the middle of the 1975-76 season.

However, he eventually redeemed his reputation when he returned to Salt Lake City five years later and repaid all who had lost money in the bankruptcy of the Stars (even though he wasn't legally obligated to do so) at a personal cost of more than $750,000.

In the early 1980s, when talk was buzzing about kicking off a new United States Football League (USFL) team, Bill couldn't resist getting involved. He put up the money to start the L.A. Express, a Los Angeles team. Bill's associate Tom Marinkovich remembered, "I spent a lot of time out there, principally writing checks, but it was fun, and we enjoyed every minute of it." After a few years, Bill could see that this venture, too, was doomed, and he wisely sold the team before the USFL folded.

Bill was never ashamed that most of his sports investments failed. He used these stories to poke fun at himself, and he always emphasized that these ventures were more about fun than business. Although he reportedly lost $200,000 in the early 1970s sponsoring the racecar driven by Lloyd Ruby in the Indianapolis

bill daniels

I'D PREFER TO MAKE IT TO THE CHAMPIONSHIPS EVERY YEAR AND NOT MAKE A DIME —

THAT IS HOW CRAZY SPORTS OWNERSHIP IS!

Bill's personalized Utah Stars championship ring. When he learned that someone had stolen a player's ring, Bill mailed this ring to the player as a replacement.

Best of luck To my very good friend Bill Lloyd Ruby

500, he later recalled, "It was an expensive hobby, but I had a ball." About his almost five percent ownership of the Lakers, he told a friend, "I prefer to make it to the championships every year and not make a dime. That is how crazy sports ownership is."

Bill's last sports investment was the Denver Grand Prix in 1990 and 1991. He lost $6 million the first year, but supported a second year at $4 million so that vendors and investors, including the City and County of Denver and the State of Colorado, could recover their investments.

"The Denver Grand Prix was good for Denver," Bill said later. "Hotels made a lot of money on it, it highlighted the city, and it was well produced. It was good for everybody but me, but that's OK." Bill succeeded in his goal of preventing any damage to Denver's fledgling reputation as a city capable of hosting world-class events.

Bill sponsored racecar driver Lloyd Ruby in the Indianapolis 500.

CHAPTER TEN

CARING, GIVING, AND MAKING LIVES BETTER: A LEGACY OF PHILANTHROPY

I ask my fellow cable friends to look for projects to support. Don't wait to be asked. Do not give to get. Give for the sake of giving.

~ Bill Daniels

When Bill Daniels took the stage to address the Atlantic Cable Show in 1989, he had an important message for his colleagues in the cable industry. It wasn't about market share or new technology or the explosion in the number of cable channels. It was about something much more important: the industry's responsibility to the community.

"What a fantastic accomplishment for our industry it would be if every single one of us did just one thing for one charitable cause this coming year," Bill told the

Microsoft founder Bill Gates shared the cover of a 2000 issue of Philanthropy *with Bill. The accompanying story highlighted their different approaches to giving.*

crowd. "I ask my fellow cable friends to look for projects to support. Don't wait to be asked. Do not give to get. Give for the sake of giving."

Another finding of the 1990 "Cable Cares" study that Bill had commissioned was that the industry had contributed approximately $5.5 billion to municipalities, charitable organizations, and disaster victims during the previous decade. Bill was proud of that number, not just for the business and political goodwill it generated, but for the simple fact that he worked with good people who wanted to do good. Bill expected his associates to give back to their communities. He even occasionally collected money in the office for an urgent need.

His own philanthropic commitments were wide-ranging and rooted in his life experience. For example, he regularly gave immediate, anonymous cash gifts to families who lost their homes in a fire or had a health emergency.

Though these people were strangers to him, when Bill learned of their needs, his heart (and his resources) went out to them. He also gave to homeless shelters and food pantries in Denver and spent time talking with the parents and children who used these services. Having grown up in the Depression and known precarious times, Bill acted quickly to help families in dire circumstances.

He also sent money to the facility where his developmentally disabled sister, Dorothy, lived in her later years after Bill's mother became too old to provide the homecare that Dorothy needed. Adele died in 1987, at the age of 92. Her death came just one year after Dorothy's. Bill admired his mother more than anyone. Throughout his life, he seemed to be striving to follow Adele's example of big-hearted generosity.

Another inspiration for Bill's philanthropy was the drive of young people to improve themselves. Perhaps he

Bill's foundation was featured in the Wall Street West section of the Rocky Mountain News.

Move-in target date is December 1997

Complex to create campus gateway to the world of business. **Page 1A**

■ **Business education goal: 'real-world perspective for real-world sucess.' Page 3A**

ROCKY MOUNTAIN NEWS

TODAY

Daniels gives DU $11 million

Generous gift spurs building plans for Daniels College of Business. **Page 1A**

A new home for the University of Denver's Daniels College of Business will rise on the southwest corner of Evans Avenue and University Boulevard, creating a new gateway to the University Park campus. The three-story portion, parallel to University Boulevard, will abut a six-story tower. This view looks toward University Boulevard from an interior quadrangle. To the left is Margery Reed Hall, which will be renovated for the hotel, restaurant and tourism program. To the right is University Hall.

Cable TV pioneer's story

Vision, entrepreneurship and humanitarianism

DENVER — Bill Daniels, cable television pioneer and Denver entrepreneur, is giving the University of Denver $11 million for construction of a new building that will house the Daniels College of Business at DU.

Current plans for the college's new home will create a prominent gateway to DU's University Park campus, with construction of a complex that will complete the southwest corner of the highly visible Evans Avenue-University Boulevard intersection in south Denver.

Daniels' gift, combined with another $11 million he gave to DU several years ago, brings his investment in the University to $22 million and sets a record in DU's philanthropic history. The Daniels College project will provide the first new academic space for DU students since the late 1960s.

A new home for the business college — one of DU's largest academic units with nearly 2,000 students — is one of the major goals of The University of Denver Campaign, a $140 million fund-raising effort launched last November. More than $79 million has been raised.

"We said then that this capital campaign would change the University of Denver in profound and enduring ways," said Chancellor Daniel L. Ritchie. "Bill Daniels' generosity assures that business students at DU will be among the first to experience that change. They will learn to be team-builders, leaders and valued members of their communities in surroundings whose quality matches the curriculum that his philosophies have helped shape."

Another $7 million will be raised to complete the estimated $18 million cost of the project. Pending continued successful fund-raising, groundbreaking is scheduled for July 1996. The move-in target is the holiday break in December 1997. "There are many business men and women on the Denver scene who have done extremely well," commented Daniels. "My hope is that they will step to the plate to provide the additional $7 million needed to complete the project." Announcement of Daniels' gift kicks off the Daniels College por-

See **DANIELS** on 3A

It made front-page news in Denver when Bill donated $11 million for the construction of a new building to house the Daniels College of Business at the University of Denver.

saw in them a bit of his own youthful spirit. He supported the training of a few amateur athletes. Both directly and through scholarships, Bill also paid for a number of men to attend New Mexico Military Institute, and put several young people through college, including relatives as well as the children of friends. In these circumstances, he embraced his role as a mentor and didn't hesitate to give advice in letters about the need to behave honorably and study hard and get involved in the community on campus.

These efforts eventually led to a very public donation in 1988. That year Bill gave an $11 million challenge grant to the University of Denver (DU) College of Business to start teaching ethics and etiquette in their MBA program. Bill lamented, "There is virtually no place in the country where young men and women can learn such basic assets as manners, protocol, communication skills, treatment of people, ethics, integrity, respect for others, dress, and all the other qualities that go toward making successful

business careers for men and women . . . In addition, few are taught at a young age the value of giving back to their community and society." The new program at DU aimed to address those shortcomings.

In recognition of Bill's generosity, the business school was renamed the Daniels College of Business in 1994. The following year, Bill gave another $11 million for the construction of new facilities.

While Bill never earned a college degree, he knew how important a formal education was to career advancement. But he also didn't want book learning and theory to overshadow practical and social skills. "I learned early in my business career that *business is people*," Bill told Dan Ritchie, DU's chancellor. Bill's gifts ensured that generations of DU students would get the people skills necessary for success.

As a businessman, Bill Daniels understood it was often necessary to spend money to make money, and he put that

Dan Ritchie (left) and Dr. Jim Griesemer were with Bill for the unveiling of the new sign when the business school at the University of Denver was renamed the Daniels College of Business.

strategy into practice philanthropically as well. Nowhere was this more obvious than at Cableland, his 19,500-square-foot home in Denver that opened in 1987 as both a residence and a venue for charitable and political fundraisers.

Bill's presence at Cableland wasn't required for millions of dollars to be raised in his residence. Often he wasn't even home when events were underway.

Cableland didn't have sufficient parking for large gatherings, so guests attending big events parked their cars on the streets near the mansion. Neighbors irritated by the inconvenience petitioned the city about it. When Bill learned what they had done, he was infuriated with his neighbors and greatly disappointed in their actions. "What I could not understand was how anybody could object to having cars parked in front of their homes if

we're raising money to feed the poor or for some other worthy cause," he reflected. "That just broke my heart."

He solved the problem by hiring valets to park cars at a nearby church, but he also wrote a letter to all the neighbors who had complained. In typical fashion, his comments were conciliatory, but pointed. "You care about peace and quiet, security and quality of life in our neighborhood," his letter said. "But let me remind you that we live in a larger neighborhood. And, unless we act in a way that demonstrates our true commitment to that larger community, many will believe we are a small neighborhood of Scrooges."

When Bill died, Cableland was donated to the City and County of Denver (as Bill had directed) to be used as the official mayoral residence and for continued use as a venue for charitable events.

ABOVE | *In 1987, Bill moved into Cableland (his 19,500-square-foot home in Denver), which he built as both a residence and a venue for charitable and political fundraisers. Cableland is designated as Denver's official mayoral residence.* OPPOSITE | *Demonstrating Bill's pride in his home state, a rug of Colorado's state seal greeted visitors entering Bill's Cableland residence.*

CHAPTER ELEVEN

FAITH, LOVE, AND LOSS: A SPIRITUAL SIDE OF A COMPLEX MAN

I say my prayers at least once a day. I thank the good Lord for the blessings He has bestowed on me and ask forgiveness for my sins. Not only have I been lucky, but the guy upstairs guided me to the right places most of the time.

~ Bill Daniels

Bill was a complex man who could hold seemingly contradictory views in comfortable proximity. He valued loyalty and perseverance but was divorced four times. He worked non-stop to build a fortune and shrugged each time he lost a good chunk of it. He excelled without a college degree but believed all young people deserved a chance to earn one. He expected people to take responsibility for themselves but was a champion of the hungry and homeless. He had high expectations for himself and others but could joke about his own failings and offered second chances when deserved.

Perhaps Bill's greatest contradiction was his tough exterior and warm heart. Beneath the scrappy boxer, fearless fighter pilot, tenacious negotiator, and champion

Bill in the Colorado mountains he loved so much.

Don't panic —

I am not born again. But the cross attached to this note is a duplicate of the one I carry in my pocket at all times.

You might consider carrying it with you. It is a symbol of my love for you guys, and we know we are all believers.

of proper conduct was a man who knew how to love, laugh, and forgive. He had a soft spot for hard-luck stories, a tenderness in the presence of pain, and an abiding faith in God's mercy.

In the last years of Bill's life, as age and illness overtook him, a spiritual peace began slowly to live simultaneously with his relentless drive. On December 24, 1995, he wrote a letter to a group of executives he had mentored. Carefully folded into each letter was a tiny aluminum cross. "Don't panic," he wrote. "I am not born again. But the cross attached to this note is a duplicate of the one I carry in my pocket at all times. You might consider carrying it with you. It is a symbol of my love for you guys, and we know we are all believers."

Over the years, Bill gave out hundreds of the small crosses to people who had meant something special to him. One was a Jewish gentleman who received the cross with an explanation from Bill. "I don't want to offend you because I know you are of the Jewish faith," Bill told him. "But crosses are very important to me and I wanted to give one to you as a reminder of me." Years later the

man admitted that he always carried the cross with him, not because it had any religious connotation for him, but because it was a gift from Bill and a reminder of their friendship.

Bill's generosity — as well as his caring and compassion — was legendary. But Bill's faith was something he kept, literally, close to his heart. Only a few people knew much about Bill's spiritual side. One of them was Methodist minister Ed Beck.

The two met around 1970 when Reverend Beck gave an invocation at an event Bill attended. Bill was impressed with the prayer and asked to be introduced to Reverend Beck so he could get a copy of it. Their conversation that night was the beginning of a friendship that would last the rest of Bill's life.

Bill's spirituality had its roots early in his childhood. Adele Davis Daniels had been an active member of a church in Hobbs. As a young boy, Bill often accompanied his mother to the services, but over time he became disenchanted with the formality and institutional framework of the church. The religious teachings that had been part of his upbringing were echoed in the messages he heard many years later in Alcoholics Anonymous and contributed to his ability to remain sober.

Though Bill rarely engaged in formal religion during his middle years, he began attending Reverend Beck's worship services in Denver after the two met. But Bill arrived only in time for the sermon and typically sat in the last pew.

In the last decade of his life, Bill suffered from hearing loss that significantly curtailed his social life and face-to-face participation in his business as well as his ability to hear the sermons. But as in every other aspect of his life, he persevered.

Bill's hearing became so impaired that people had to shout in order for Bill to hear them, either in person or on the telephone. But he wasn't ashamed of his disability, just intensely frustrated by it. When he gave presentations, he addressed his disability honestly and openly. "I have a severe hearing problem," he told students at Casper College, "and as a result of that it's hard for me to visit with people. If my hearing was normal, I'd like to visit with every one of you, but that ain't gonna happen because I can't hear you."

As Bill got older, his medical issues became much more severe than a hearing disability. The first of a cascading series of life-threatening health episodes occurred in March of 1996 when Bill experienced pain so severe he called one of his longtime friends in the medical field who implored him to seek help immediately. Finally convinced that his situation might be more than a transient problem, Bill went to the emergency room at Eisenhower Medical Center in Rancho Mirage, California, where he was diagnosed with diverticulitis. The top-flight doctors who saved his life estimated that he was close to death when he arrived at the hospital.

Many people believe this episode, and the resulting five months he spent in the hospital, gave Bill a different perspective of his own faith and mortality as well as the motivation to begin serious plans for his foundation. Had his friend not persuaded Bill to seek medical care immediately, some wonder whether the Daniels Fund would be in existence today.

In his last few years, he was also challenged by severe respiratory problems that made it hard to breathe in high-altitude Denver, so he stayed mostly in his California home, far from most of his friends and associates. He continued to review reports and meeting minutes sent by associates, mentor young people through letters of encouragement, and share his appreciation of lifelong friends by sending them kind notes.

COURTESY OF BARCO LIBRARY, THE CABLE CENTER

During these later years, Bill and Reverend Beck had increasingly open and revealing conversations where Bill explored his deep-seated questions of faith and religion. Bill began to refer to Reverend Beck as his "spiritual advisor."

"I say my prayers at least once a day," he wrote to a friend. "I thank the good Lord for the blessings He has bestowed on me and ask forgiveness for my sins."

He acknowledged, "Not only have I been lucky, but the guy upstairs guided me to the right places most of the time."

Bill took solace in the Bible and the view from his home of a lighted cross on a hill in Lake San Marcos, California. Bill owned the land where the cross was erected, and made sure that it was lighted and maintained for the whole community to enjoy.

About 18 months before his death, Bill unexpectedly quizzed his longtime pilot Mark Calkins about Mark's faith. Though the question took him by surprise, Mark explained his beliefs in some detail, then looked to his boss for a reaction. Bill responded, "I believe *all* of that!"

Flying back to Palm Springs about a year before his death, Bill had a heart attack on the airplane. His condition was grave, but he pulled through and spent several months recuperating at the Eisenhower Medical Center.

Persuading the doctors to release him for a few hours, Bill called Reverend Beck and asked to meet him at the

Mark Calkins (right) was Bill's longtime pilot.

airport in Scottsdale. "The doctors think it's a miracle I'm alive," Bill told the minister in their brief, one-hour meeting. "Why do you think God let me live?"

Reverend Beck's response was, "My theory is that God has given you some extra time . . . because there is something vitally important that you need to do and it's not done." When he asked Bill what that might be, Bill answered without any hesitation. "My foundation." Though Bill said that the foundation was "already together," there were certain things that he still wanted to do with it.

Reverend Beck gave him encouragement. "I believe that God has given you borrowed time to get your dream fulfilled," he told Bill. "Because the foundation is going to be extremely helpful for a lot of people who have never known Bill Daniels but will know his legacy."

With his energy waning, Bill spent much of his last year finalizing plans for the foundation that would carry his name and his billion-dollar fortune for years to come. He made decisions about funding college scholarships and supporting certain causes, and he put together the foundation's first board. The Daniels Fund would be one of the largest foundations in the Rocky Mountain region.

As the plans for the foundation were completed, Bill told his minister and friend that he felt that a weight had been lifted from his shoulders, and he was ready to answer God's final call.

Bill Daniels died on March 7, 2000.

The front-page articles in newspapers around the country mentioned the many awards and honors he received over the years, including Denver Humanitarian of the Year, the Will Rogers Memorial Award from the New Mexico Military Institute, induction into the Colorado Business Hall of Fame and the Cable Television Hall of Fame, and a special Emmy award for his role in the development of television.

Probably more significant to Bill would have been the many glowing remarks that his friends, colleagues, and associates made about him in multiple memorial services

Bill considered Reverend Ed Beck his "spiritual advisor" and friend. When plans for Bill's foundation were completed near the end of his life, he flew to Scottsdale. The two men are pictured in Bill's Learjet.

celebrating his life. They called him one of the finest people they'd ever known, a giant in the community, and an example of what is best in humanity.

Perhaps one of the most fitting accolades about Bill was one offered by President Gerald Ford.

"In America, anyone can grow up to be president," he said. "But not everyone can grow up to be a Bill Daniels. I wish there were more like him."

Undoubtedly, Bill would have felt a sense of pride and humility in hearing the heartfelt comments about him. But, more important, he would have also felt a sense of peace and accomplishment in knowing that because of his wealth, generosity, and faith, the gifts he bestowed would make a difference in people's lives forever.

That is the legacy of Bill Daniels.

USED BY PERMISSION, SCRIPPS MEDIA, INC.

USED BY PERMISSION, THE DENVER POST

OPPOSITE | *Bill, captured in a reflective moment.* ABOVE | *After Bill died on March 7, 2000, his life was lauded in newspapers around the country.*

THE
DANIELS FUND

CHAPTER TWELVE

A LIFE BECOMES A LEGACY

I spend most of my time these days making the decisions about my foundation that will provide, I believe, a huge advance in our society.

~ Bill Daniels

In 1995, at age 74, Bill Daniels wrote a letter to Malcolm S. Forbes, Jr., president and editor-in-chief of *Forbes* magazine. Wrote Bill,

Every year you publish a list of the 400 richest people in America. While I've been included for several years, I've never considered wealth as the primary measure of my success. For me, the biggest kick I get out of life is giving back to those less fortunate and using money to do good things for people. Wouldn't it make a marvelous statement to business people throughout the country if you included in your tally of each of "the 400's" net worth the amount they have donated to philanthropic causes each year? All of us, including your editors, need to find creative ways to reinforce the value of helping those in need.

The Denver headquarters of the Daniels Fund were completed in 2003 in Bill's beloved Cherry Creek neighborhood near his home. Bill chose the site himself before he died.

Throughout his life, Bill Daniels demonstrated his commitment to helping others and giving back. He gave generously to individuals in crisis and to nonprofit organizations that served people down on their luck. He supported athletic programs for youth, ethics education for business students, and financial literacy programs through his unique Young Americans Bank. He paid to send young people to college and donated to numerous educational institutions, many times in the names of friends and colleagues.

In addition to sharing his wealth, Bill got involved with those he helped — visiting with prisoners, guiding college students, serving on a nonprofit board, talking with homeless families. Perhaps most important, he encouraged others to give. He was an example to the associates in his companies to make their own community contributions. He lectured his colleagues in the cable industry to do their part to give back. And whenever he advised young people, he included a message about volunteering and contributing.

When Bill was in his seventies and his health began to decline, he faced mortality with his typical forthright determination. Knowing his window of opportunity was narrowing, Bill began defining the specifics of his foundation and its operations with renewed focus. Adding to the sense of urgency was the unexpected death of one of Bill's close friends with a large estate but no prepared plan of what should be done with it. The public and bitter legal feud that resulted — plus millions forfeited to taxes — was appalling to Bill, who felt that those millions could have been better spent. It was a wake-up call, and he became even more determined not to have the same thing happen when he died.

With the help of his attorneys, Bill undertook plans for a grant-making foundation that would last for generations to come. Five months before his death, Bill wrote, "I spend most of my time these days making the decisions about my foundation that will provide, I believe, a huge advance in our society."

It was not an easy task to make binding decisions about how his money would be spent in the future, but he cared deeply about those decisions and the people who would benefit from his generosity. Each decision was made with a great deal of thought and with specific directives that could not be changed.

Bill outlined his giving priorities in a set of foundation bylaws that will always guide the Daniels Fund. For the most part, these interests were represented in Bill's charitable giving throughout his life. The basic areas he wished to fund were clear and are now addressed by these funding areas:

- ✦ Scholarships for College
- ✦ Grant Funding Areas
    - ✦ Aging
    - ✦ Alcoholism and Substance Abuse
    - ✦ Amateur Sports
    - ✦ Disabilities
    - ✦ Early Childhood Education
    - ✦ K-12 Education Reform

A timeline of major events in Bill's life — tracing his story from his death in 2000 to his birth in 1920 — runs along the walls of several meeting rooms at the Daniels Fund.

- ✦ Ethics and Integrity in Education
- ✦ Homeless and Disadvantaged
  - ✦ Rapid Response
- ✦ Youth Development
- ✦ Young Americans Bank

The bylaws he created directed that approximately 30 percent of charitable allocations would support college scholarships, with the remainder going to grants. Bill also defined the geographic areas where he wished his money directed: 75 percent of scholarship funding would be for students from Colorado, 10 percent for students from New Mexico, 10 percent for students from Wyoming, and 5 percent for students from Utah. Of the grant allocations, 50 percent was directed to the Denver Metro area, 15 percent to other areas in Colorado, 25 percent in total to New Mexico, Wyoming, and Utah, and 10 percent to national programs.

Bill clarified that these four states "contributed to the luck I have had." Colorado was his primary home most of his adult life and the location of his business headquarters. He lived in Hobbs, New Mexico, as a teen and attended the New Mexico Military Institute, which was a key factor in his future success. Wyoming was the location of his first cable system, which catapulted his career. And Utah claimed a special place in Bill's heart when he made Salt Lake City the new home of his first professional basketball team, the American Basketball Association's Utah Stars.

As his plans progressed, Bill selected the first board of directors for the foundation. He communicated some of his expectations directly to them. "Please remember that I am a conservative," he wrote the board members.

Bill believed in conservative Republican tenets such as fiscal responsibility, limited government, and programs that honor a "hand up, not a hand out." He did not like entitlement programs.

The bylaws also specified areas that Bill *did not* wish to support. He prohibited support of "research of any kind," probably because he always gave to programs that actively worked to help people, not to programs that analyzed how to prevent problems. He also prohibited funding for the treatment of AIDS, because he knew his resources could not make a sizable impact on this global problem and that it was a focus for numerous other foundations.

Bill was particularly adamant that he did not want his foundation to give to cultural activities. Although he allowed that up to one percent of allocations *could* be used for cultural purposes in Denver if something special came up, his restriction was in keeping with his priorities during his lifetime. "Most of my giving just does not match with symphonies, art, and opera," Bill wrote. "I am just not into that. I am into helping people who need help, who are hungry, unclothed, in trouble . . . In my case, I am for the underdog, for guys who need a second chance."

In 1997, Bill hired Phil Hogue, former president of Daniels & Associates, to help make the plans for the foundation operational. Bill's death marked the beginning of the Daniels Fund.

The board members — who were all people close to Bill — worked in earnest to fulfill Bill's wishes.

The scholarship and grant guidelines and application procedures were developed, a staff was hired, and foundation facilities were built.

Even while these decisions were being made, funding was distributed so as not to delay the impact Bill wanted to have. By May of 2000, the first grants had been awarded in Colorado, and the first class of 32 Daniels Scholars was named, in time to support their first year of college the following fall.

The board of directors was busy, but it was an honor to be part of building an important legacy that would make a significant difference in people's lives. After the transfer of $1.1 billion from Bill's estate, the Daniels Fund became the largest foundation in the Rocky Mountain region and one of the 50 largest foundations in the country.

Despite much progress, translating Bill's directives and turning them into complex programs serving a four-state region was daunting. Dozens of accomplished professionals with philanthropy backgrounds were hired. They knew the nonprofit world, but were unfamiliar with Bill's personal style of giving. Adding to the emerging challenges, satellite offices that had been established in each state represented Bill's vision to varying degrees.

Within the first two years of operation, the board realized it had lost control of donor intent. "It didn't take all that long, but all of a sudden the Daniels Fund was starting to look like someone else's foundation," said Linda Childears, president and CEO of the Daniels Fund. The board took action, to ensure Bill's vision and wishes would be upheld, just as he would have demanded.

There were challenges. The board found that in many ways his wishes were very explicit, but he didn't leave much guidance for the *principles* that should govern the Daniels Fund's grant-making.

"I don't think the donor — as smart as he was and as much time and attention as he gave to his plan over the last two years in his life — had any idea of the complexity of implementing his plan," reflected John Saeman, who became board chairman of the Daniels Fund in 2003.

To better interpret and define Bill's wishes, the board began a painstaking review of nearly 60 years of Bill's business and personal correspondence. The review encompassed speeches, documents detailing Bill's personal philanthropy, and letters he sent with those gifts. To get an even broader perspective, numerous people who knew Bill were interviewed to better understand what he wanted the Daniels Fund to accomplish in each area he identified.

After compiling and analyzing all those materials, the Daniels Fund Board developed a thorough set of documents describing Bill's principles and what he wanted to accomplish with his money. These documents are critical tools for those committed to honoring Bill's legacy and furthering his example of compassion, ethics, and integrity. In making the many decisions that board members face, they are guided by some final words Bill spoke on his convictions:

I think God told me as a young man to share my good fortune with others. I have tried to do it. And my foundation will see to it when I die. Believe me, it is a real joy to me to be able to help people.

OPPOSITE | *Bill in the Daniels Communications Center.* Courtesy of Barco Library, The Cable Center

PART THREE

SCHOLARSHIPS

CHAPTER THIRTEEN

SCHOLARSHIPS FOR COLLEGE

If you've never taken a chance on yourself, at least think about it. Unless you do, you may never know what you're missing out on. And neither will the rest of the world.

~Bill Daniels

Daniels Scholarships are awarded each spring to graduating high school seniors to help them complete an undergraduate degree.

Bill's Story

When Bill Daniels agreed to pay for the college education of a friend's son, he wrote the young man a letter, clarifying "some caveats" of the offer. In the letter, Bill clearly outlined his expectations about grades, conduct, and involvement in student affairs. A *verbal* confirmation that he was meeting his obligations wouldn't be enough. The student was expected to submit a monthly *written* progress report as well as a copy of his grades each term.

"The point I am making is that you will have to perform," Bill wrote. "I am a tough taskmaster, especially when it comes to young people, but I can't tell you the pride I have watching the success of most of the young

After receiving an honorary doctorate from Rocky Mountain College in Billings, Montana, Bill is joined by the college's former president, Bruce Alton (left) and former chairman of the board of trustees, Robert Nance (right).

This past week, for some reason, I have received 4 letters from alumni, all thanking me for things I have taught them —

I guess one just fails to realize the impact they have on young people. That is the one legacy I will be proudest to leave.

people I have tried to help. You can do it! I am betting on you."

Bill bet on a lot of young men and women over the years. By 1992 he had already funded the college educations of many young people. "I enjoy sharing my good fortune with others, most especially young people with talent and drive," he wrote. "It's a good feeling to be able to help students who really need it."

Some of those he helped openly; others he helped behind the scenes. Since Bill's death in 2000, the Daniels Fund has discovered that Bill established more than 15 endowments in honor of his friends and associates. Beyond the provisions of his foundation, these endowments were further proof of his commitment in this area.

When Bill was in high school in the 1930s, a college education was not viewed as essential for professional success. He completed two years of junior college at the New Mexico Military Institute (where he graduated from high school), but then World War II intervened and

he became a fighter pilot. Once the war was over, Bill returned home and joined the family insurance business. College was put on indefinite hold.

Despite his extraordinarily successful career, Bill was sometimes self-conscious about not having a degree, especially when speaking at universities. But he was open and emphatic in stressing the importance of a college education for others. "I had zilch formal business education," he told students at Casper College. "The only reason I'm telling you that is, as lucky and as fortunate as I was, think what you'll do if you get a formal education."

When he spoke to a group of students at Dartmouth's Tuck School of Business, he confessed, "I never had an accounting course in my life. When I went into business, I didn't know what a balance sheet was, and I didn't know what a profit and loss statement was. I promise you I know now, but I learned the hard way. I could have saved a lot of time. If I had to do it over again, I would get an undergraduate degree, and I would get an MBA."

Bill occasionally poked fun at the limits of his own education to drive home his message. When he was decades into his career, he told the Dartmouth students about when he and an associate were at a meeting where someone used the term *quid pro quo*. As the two colleagues left the meeting, Bill asked his friend, "What did that guy mean by *quid pro quo*? I thought he was talking about an octopus." Though his comment may have been in jest, the point of his story was serious.

With an insatiable hunger for knowledge, Bill never hesitated to ask questions and probe for answers. Most days, he was up by four o'clock in the morning, reading five or more newspapers with his morning coffee. Any subject that caught his eye was diligently researched and explored.

Whenever Bill helped individuals go to college, he provided more than financial support; he also mentored them through the process with encouraging words and advice. His requirement that they write to him regularly

was not just about holding the students accountable, but about keeping informed of potential stumbling blocks he could help them overcome.

Three years before his death, Bill wrote to a longtime associate. "The past week, for some reason, I have received four letters from alumni all thanking me for things I have taught them," Bill said. "I guess one just fails to realize the impact they have on young people. That is the one legacy I will be proudest to leave."

June Travis, a cable industry colleague, reflected on Bill's ability to find kids who were at risk of falling through the cracks unless they had some help. Said June, "He had an innate ability to do that, to look at people and see one spark, regardless of their background. Then he'd invest in them personally and watch them succeed, and that gave him great joy."

Another colleague, Steve Schuck, echoed those sentiments. "Bill Daniels just loved young people, and

he was so committed to improving the quality of their lives. If he could interact with the Daniels Scholars of today, I'm sure he would simply say, 'Take advantage of this opportunity. I am proud of you. I am happy for you. I want what's best for you. Choose your course and make a total commitment to it, and when you're all done, give something back to somebody else, to those who follow.' "

Today, Bill's legacy of giving young people financial support, as well as encouragement and advice, is solidified by the Daniels Fund honoring Bill's direction to allocate approximately 30 percent of its annual distributions to scholarships. Bill specified that this support should help students of high character who, though they might not have the highest grades or test scores, showed great potential.

As Bill planned the scholarship component of the Daniels Fund, he had great visions of a "pay it forward"

The 2008 class of Daniels Scholars poses in front of the Daniels Fund headquarters in Denver.

philosophy. "When these kids graduate," said Bill, "they will graduate and then go back and help their community. They will go out and mentor the next group, and it will continue on and on and on."

Putting Bill's Wishes into Practice

Always focused on Bill's desire to encourage young people to believe in themselves and give the world their best shot, the Daniels Fund began awarding scholarships just months after Bill's death. It was what Bill would have wanted.

Daniels Scholarships are designed to create opportunities for young men and women in Colorado, New Mexico, Utah, and Wyoming who possess certain characteristics identified by Bill Daniels. He directed that scholarship recipients should be well-rounded people with leadership potential who embrace the chance to learn, adhere to high ethical standards, are committed to working hard to earn a bachelor's degree, and who welcome the joy of giving back to their communities and families, just as Bill would have expected.

The scholarship covers unmet financial needs after all other financial resources have been applied. Scholarship amounts are different for each student and can change from year to year.

In keeping with Bill Daniels' high expectations of the students he supported, Daniels Scholars must meet ongoing requirements: maintain satisfactory grades and progress toward degree completion, adhere to the *Daniels Scholar Code of Conduct*, and submit an annual "personal evaluation." They are also required to live on campus in their freshman year and to hold a job during each academic year.

Daniels Scholars receive more than financial aid. They become part of a community of people who all care about their success. Before heading to college, new Daniels Scholars come together at an orientation where they meet one another, develop support systems, and

Daniels Scholars spend time together during a scholarship orientation program.

learn more about the scholarship program. They also learn more about the high standards Bill expected of himself and others: ethics and integrity, etiquette and communication skills, financial responsibility, civic engagement, and giving back.

Throughout their college years, Daniels Scholars work with staff members at the Daniels Fund who offer encouragement, guide them to resources on campus, and monitor their progress. Scholars are also urged to take advantage of programs focused on building life skills that will have long-term impact.

Daniels Fund involvement with the Scholars doesn't end at graduation. After Scholars earn their degrees, the goal is for them to join a network of Daniels Scholars Alumni all over the world who are connected through encouragement from the Daniels Fund.

Success was a driving force in Bill Daniels' life. Just as Bill knew that there are many ways to measure it, the same is true for the Daniels Fund, which measures success in a number of ways. The ultimate goal to Bill was that students become productive, engaged members of society. Many Daniels Scholars are the first members of their families to attend college. The group reflects the ethnic diversity of the Daniels Fund's four-state region.

With a record of achievement spanning many years, Daniels Scholars have become highly productive members of society who have made an impact on their communities and the wider world. Pick any career field and there is likely a Daniels Scholar forging ahead in it. Some have followed in Bill's footsteps as entrepreneurs and business leaders. Others have become engineers, teachers, pharmacists, reporters, physical therapists, elected officials, nurses, and software developers.

In addition to the traditional Daniels Scholarships, the Daniels Fund may also provide financial assistance to students who don't necessarily follow a traditional high school-to-college educational path. For instance, recipients might be GED recipients, youth who have been in foster care programs or juvenile justice facilities, returning military personnel, or individuals pursuing EMT / paramedic training.

Bill wanted those motivated enough to pursue an education to have a chance at getting one, regardless of their backgrounds.

The 2009 class of Daniels Scholars gathers for a group photo during orientation at the University of Denver.

PART FOUR

GRANT FUNDING AREAS

CHAPTER FOURTEEN

AGING

My greatest hero was my mother. She was the loveliest person I have ever known. I absolutely adored her."

~ Bill Daniels

The Daniels Fund supports programs that assist older adults in achieving maximum independence and quality of life through in-home services, community engagement, and end-of-life / palliative care.

Bill's Story

Bill's motivation to fund this grant area was greatly influenced by the care and concern that he had for his mother. People who knew him said that

Adele Davis Daniels was the person whom Bill admired more than anyone else on earth.

Born into a prominent and respected family, Adele trained as a teacher. But her real passion was the arts, which she pursued through acting. At one time, she was on the playbill with a young thespian named Henry Fonda and rubbed shoulders with the likes of Jimmy Stewart and other rising actors.

Through good times and bad, Adele was willing to help when anyone needed her, and held the family together through triumph and tragedy. She watched

Bill's mother, Adele, was always the most important woman in his life.

Bill go off to two wars, endured her husband's untimely death, and took care of her developmentally disabled daughter, Dorothy.

Through it all, she maintained a sense of humor and a commanding presence. Known for her straight talking, she didn't mince words when Bill's brother, Jack, encouraged her to attend one of Bill's weddings. "If we went out of town every time Bill got married, we'd all be broke," she said with characteristic wit and directness.

Adele had a profound influence on Bill's life, and no doubt he inherited some of her strong traits. Though they lived miles apart, Bill made visiting her as often as possible a top priority. In between visits, they kept close tabs on each other by phone. Night or day, Adele enjoyed hearing from her son. Even when she was in her eighties, and even if it was after midnight, Bill might call her to give her some news, or tell her about the woman he was seeing. Sometimes he even put his date on the phone to "meet" his mother.

He also loved to share his business successes with her. On the day he learned that Mile High Cablevision — a company in which Bill was a major shareholder — had been awarded the hard-fought contract to install Denver's first-ever cable service, Bill excused himself from the celebration. His first priority was to call his 88-year-old mother, who shed tears of joy as he told her the good news. She knew that they had been trying to get this contract for 25 years.

As his mother eased from her eighties into her nineties, Bill understood that she didn't want to leave her own home in Hobbs, so he made sure she had everything she needed for safety and comfort and continued to see her as often as possible. During those visits, Bill often took Adele to their favorite family restaurant, George's, where they were served by their favorite waitress, Wilma Voorhies. Wilma had worked at George's for years and knew all the members of the Daniels family.

When Adele Daniels died in 1987 at the age of 92, her death was a blow to the devoted son. "I absolutely adored her," Bill wrote a friend years later. "As a matter of fact, Mother's Day is the toughest day of the year for me." Less than two months before his own death, Bill wrote another friend about his mother, "My greatest hero was my mother. She was the loveliest person I have ever known."

Ten years after Adele's death, Wilma Voorhies opened her mailbox in Hobbs to find a Christmas card from Bill Daniels. This was no surprise, as Bill had remembered to send a card to his favorite waitress every Christmas for years. He had great respect for how hard a waitress works, and he continued to stay in touch with Wilma even though he no longer visited Hobbs. It was near the end of Bill's life — when Wilma must have been getting on in years herself — that she opened Bill's Christmas card to find a check for $10,000. By this time she had retired, and Bill told Wilma in the card to expect the same amount every year for the rest of her life. He wanted her to have a comfortable retirement after all those years on her feet waiting tables. Amazingly, Bill's generosity came full circle when Wilma directed in her will that the remaining portion of Bill's monetary gift be returned upon her death to the Daniels Fund. After she died, the Daniels Fund received a check for $90,000.

Bill's gift to Wilma was indicative of his constant concern for the wellbeing of others, especially when sickness and age were getting the better of them. He encouraged others to take care of the elderly, too. In a Christmas message, he said, "Why not use this holiday season to demonstrate your individuality by sharing your good fortune with those around you? Take an hour out of your schedule and pay a visit to an elderly neighbor."

His sympathy is also evident in the letters he sent to aging friends. In 1987, he wrote to an elderly friend of his parents, after visiting her in a nursing home in Lakewood, Colorado. "It kills me to see you as immobile as you are," said Bill, "but I also sense that you are getting good care and you are content as can be under the circumstances. We miss you and love you."

BILL DANIELS

Mom, Sweetheart,

I wouldn't know how it feels to own anything that is not mortgaged but may I share with you the satisfaction that you will have in not having a mortgage on your cute little hacienda.

Who would have thought that, when Jack and I were snot-nosed kids, someday we could do things like this for you. Hope this helps make up for the diaper changes, the trouble I gave you and to thank you for the many peanut butter and jelly sandwiches that you labored over so long!

Love you,

It gave Bill great pleasure to be able to announce to his mother that she would no longer need to worry about a mortgage on her house.

In 1993, he wrote to another friend:

I know that you have been ill and that the past few years haven't been easy for you. Retirement is supposed to be a relaxed time of your life, but it ain't always that way. Bad things happen to good people — that isn't the way it should be, but it is sometimes . . . I know it is hard for you to write, but hopefully you will keep in touch with me. If there is anything I can ever do for you, please let me know. You have been a good friend, and I treasure our friendship. You will have some "down" days, and that is to be expected. Hopefully you can count your blessings when that happens and find some good in life.

As Bill got older, he faced his challenges. Losing his hearing was one of the most troubling issues for Bill, but that was not the worst of his health woes. In the mid-1990s, he suffered through pneumonia, severe infection, kidney failure, and blood poisoning in a cascading series of medical problems. In March of 1996, he needed emergency surgery that resulted in a colostomy. He nearly died on the operating table after his heart stopped beating and his lungs filled with fluid. The next three months of his life were spent in a hospital room at the Eisenhower Medical Center.

As soon as he was well enough to begin complaining, Bill pleaded with the doctor to reverse the colostomy. Bill's persistence wore down the doctor, who finally agreed. The operation was a success and eventually Bill was settled back in his beach house in Del Mar, California. Decades of heavy smoking had eaten away at Bill's respiratory system, making it so hard to breathe in high-altitude Denver that he stayed almost entirely in California.

No longer able to navigate stairs easily, Bill started using the smaller, single-level guesthouse on his property. He was walking every day and getting his strength back

bill daniels

I CONTINUE TO SAY I AM TAKING IT GRACEFULLY, BUT I AM REALLY PISSED OFF THAT I'M OLD.

but having difficulty gaining weight. He relied heavily on his housekeeper, his in-home nurse, and on his longtime assistant, Jayne Mitchell.

Occasionally, his spirits plummeted. In August of 1997, Bill wrote to his Navy buddy Donal "Broe" Broesamle. "I suffer mostly from being down in the dumps and all of a sudden not being able to do the things I did for so many years," Bill said. "Need I say more?"

He put it another way in a letter to another lifelong friend, Bob Delbridge. "Frank Sinatra was one of my original partners in the Palm Springs cable system," Bill said. "I knew him for many years. Not only did he say, 'It's been a hell of a ride,' he said, 'Live it up when you can, my friend, because dying is a pain in the ass.'" Sinatra's quip resonated with Bill, and he never forgot it.

While he tried to remain positive and engaged in life, Bill clearly had trouble accepting the aging process. "If you want to know what it's like later on in life, you wish you were 40 years younger," said Bill in a letter to a friend. "Believe me, I continue to say I am taking it gracefully, but I am really pissed off that I am old. Still, I had a *hell of a ride* and am a very fortunate guy." Picking up on Bill's frustration — and making light of it in a way Bill loved — Jayne gave him a throw pillow embroidered with the phrase, "Screw the golden years!"

Even with the challenges of the "golden years," Bill still had much to offer, and his colleagues recognized that. They visited him as often as they could, in part to share their friendship and respect, and in part to seek out the wisdom and advice that Bill had accumulated in a lifetime of deals and successes and failures.

As his health, hearing, and strength ebbed in the late 1990s, Bill continued to monitor the world via cable television. When his health permitted, he called friends around the nation and wrote them notes. At times he talked openly about his life and theirs, and he didn't shy away from talking about the roller-coaster ride of health that marked his final days.

In his last months, Bill said he felt like a "prisoner" in his own home. "I have to stay close to my oxygen, and I see very few people. I talk less and less on the phone other than to my staff, maybe twice a week . . . I find myself losing the old momentum I have had all of my life. I'm sure it's a part of getting old and not being in perfect health."

On a better day, he wrote to his friend Letitia Baldrige, "I can't complain. I have had a marvelous career and I am at peace with myself and feeling good."

Bill felt more at peace as he began to finalize plans for the Daniels Fund and clarify his intentions for how the foundation's money would be disbursed. He believed that God had saved him on that operating table so he could come back and do a little more good at the end of his life. His foundation plans were the culmination of his life's work, and he knew he was fortunate to have lived long enough to accomplish that mission. The Daniels Fund is committed to carrying out that mission.

COURTESY OF VIA MOBILITY SERVICES (FORMERLY SPECIAL TRANSIT)

Putting Bill's Wishes into Practice

Bill's concern for family and friends who were aging, and his honest portrayal of his own aging and illness, provide a solid understanding of his intention for Daniels Fund grants that assist older adults.

Bill knew the aging process was no easy journey. He saw that it could be physically limiting, socially isolating, and emotionally discouraging. He also knew that such challenges could be eased with the right kinds of assistance. He wanted to help other seniors maintain their dignity and remain independent.

In his later years, the limitations of Bill's poor health were kept in check by adjustments he made at home and by employing in-home nursing services. He was glad to be able to stay in his own home, where he felt most comfortable and at peace. He knew most seniors could not afford the kind of help he obtained.

As a result, the Daniels Fund supports in-home services for the elderly that help them maintain independence and stay in their own homes as long as possible. Such services include meal preparation, transportation, visiting nurses, training and time off for family caregivers, and modifications to keep a person's home safe and accessible.

The Daniels Fund supports programs offering transportation services to help older adults remain active and connect with their communities.

The Daniels Fund also prioritizes programs that enhance community engagement for older people. Like many older people whose worlds become smaller as they age, Bill fought the loneliness that accompanies the loss of community. He knew how important friendship was when he was down in the dumps, and he was fortunate to have a lot of friends who kept in touch. He also stayed involved in the work that had always given his life purpose.

While not all seniors have easy access to a network of friends and supporters, the Daniels Fund recognizes that participation in organized activities can create a sense of community and worth in older adults. Therefore, funds are available for intergenerational programs, senior volunteer programs, and other activities that bring seniors together with others for a shared, meaningful purpose.

Finally, the Daniels Fund supports end-of-life and palliative care for hospice patients and their families. In Bill's final days, he had the support and care he needed at home and in the hospital to make his passing as comfortable and pain free as possible. Until the very end, he was calling the shots about his medical treatment and funeral arrangements.

Bill Daniels demonstrated how life can end with dignity and peace. The Daniels Fund seeks to extend this legacy to others.

Support for programs that offer meal delivery and food preparation is one of the ways the Daniels Fund helps older adults remain independent.

CHAPTER FIFTEEN

ALCOHOLISM AND SUBSTANCE ABUSE

If you're gonna gamble, gamble on somebody who needs a second chance.

~ Bill Daniels

PHOTO BY NICHOLAS DeSCIOSE

The Daniels Fund supports programs that assist youth and adults with alcohol and substance abuse challenges in achieving and maintaining stability in their lives through prevention, treatment, and supportive / after-care programs.

Bill's Story

The temperature was a searing 100 degrees the day Bill Daniels emerged from the Betty Ford Center in Rancho Mirage, California. It was May 14, 1985, and, despite the oppressive heat, there was reason for optimism. Bill, at 64 years old, hadn't taken a drink in six weeks, and he was healthier than he had been in many years. The road ahead looked promising.

As he left the Center, he reflected on how far he had come since his friends and brother had persuaded him to go there weeks earlier. But he also knew that the hard work had only just begun. In rehab, his world had been carefully structured and guided. Now he was rejoining the real world with all its temptations and challenges. Bill had always been a man of great discipline and resolve, but staying sober would take all the willpower and perseverance he'd ever had.

Displaying the contrast between a check scribbled in desperation in one hand and a Betty Ford Center medallion in the other, Bill showed just how far he had come.

IS BUSINESS BUNGLING ITS BATTLE WITH BOOZE?

Cutbacks in programs for alcoholic employees could cost companies in the long run

By almost any measure, Bill Daniels is one of the most successful men of his generation. A pioneer in cable television, he has built a $1.9 billion cable and mobile communications empire and amassed a personal fortune estimated at $325 million. But a few years ago, Daniels came close to losing it all to alcohol.

Daniels, now 70, had been drinking heavily since his forties. "I drank every night," he recalls, "and then I started to leave the office earlier" to hit the sauce. Even so, Daniels kept telling himself he was fine. Then, after reaching bottom in 1985 in a Scottsdale (Ariz.) hotel room, where he drank two fifths of scotch in one night, Daniels called his secretary for help. Later that day, his two top lieutenants arrived in the corporate jet and took Daniels to the famed Betty Ford Center in Rancho Mirage, Calif. He had six weeks of intensive treatment and has been sober ever since. Moreover, he has taken his career to new heights, including founding Prime Network, the nation's largest regional cable sports network.

Booze is the substance most abused in the business world. Experts estimate

BILL DANIELS AT THE BETTY FORD CENTER: THE CABLE-TV PIONEER HAS BEEN SOBER EVER SINCE HIS 1985 TREATMENT

that it afflicts at least 10% of senior executives, such as Daniels. And of the $86 billion-plus that alcoholism costs the nation every year (table), business pays the lion's share in extra health care, lost productivity, and absenteeism.

Employee assistance programs (EAPs), designed to help workers and their families cope with personal problems that interfere with work performance, prolif-

erated in the 1980s. Today, more than 70% of the nation's largest companies offer EAPS that include help for alcoholics (table). But as corporations seek to cut health care costs, recovery programs are often the first to feel the pinch. While few companies have wiped out benefits entirely, many have asked their insurers to "manage" usage. A. Foster Higgins & Co., a benefits consulting firm, reports that 87% of 2,000 employers it surveyed now limit substance-abuse and mental-health benefits, up from 75% in 1988.

Over the long term, however, that quick-fix approach to the high costs of problem drinking may be as bad for business as for drinkers. Treatment is expensive, but it's usually a onetime charge. Many companies have learned that skirting the problem or skimping on treatment means paying full price, in salary and benefits, for a less than fully functional employee—sometimes for years.

Alcoholism affects employees at every level, but it's costliest at the top. "I don't know of anything else that has a more deleterious impact on upper management," says retired Kemper National Insurance Cos. CEO James Kemper, a re-

ALCOHOLISM REMAINS DANGEROUSLY WIDESPREAD...

DATA: NATIONAL COUNCIL ON ALCOHOLISM & DRUG DEPENDENCE

| Around 18 million Americans have a serious drinking problem | ▪ Annual deaths due to alcohol number about 105,000 | Of all hospitalized patients, 25% have alcohol-related problems | ▪ Alcohol is involved in 47% of industrial accidents | Half of all auto fatalities are due to DWI crashes, 23,352 in 1988 |

Unlike many people in his era, Bill was upfront about his battles with alcoholism.

Alcohol had long been a part of Bill's lifestyle. After all, the iconic story of Bill's career in cable television begins with his stop in 1952 for a beer and sandwich at Murphy's Bar in Denver, where he watched television for the first time. For the next 30 years, drinking was an integral part of his active social life in a business culture where three-martini lunches were the norm.

Conventions hosted by the National Cable Television Association (of which Bill had served as president) attracted people from around the country who were eager to wheel and deal over a few drinks. Lavish, well-stocked hospitality suites that Bill's company hosted were among the most popular events of the convention.

Most of the time, Bill didn't let his drinking interfere with his responsibilities, but there were some eye-opening exceptions. His first wake-up call was the night he spent in jail for driving under the influence. Around 1980 he was headed home to Del Mar, California, from a yacht party in Newport Beach when an officer stopped him. "All I had on were my shorts and a tank top, no shoes, no socks," Bill told a group of Dartmouth business students years later. Such an image is in sharp contrast to Bill's typically impeccable appearance in finely tailored suits and shoes from Neiman Marcus.

"I had two drinks for the road," Bill continued. "And I was having trouble staying on the highway. I was driving real careful. I got picked up and thrown in the can in San Diego. I was there eight hours. Talk about instant humility . . . It was a miserable experience."

However, it wasn't quite humbling and miserable enough to make him want to change his ways. "I have a long-term relationship with the Colorado and California highway patrols," Bill admitted. Over the next few years, Bill had three other episodes with drunk driving, a pattern that began to disturb him greatly.

But the pivotal event occurred in March of 1985. He'd left his home in Del Mar, and headed east. No one heard from him for several days. Eventually, a police officer found Bill sitting in a ditch, his car wrecked. Promising to

call a tow truck, the officer left Bill alone while he tended to a worse wreck down the road. In Bill's typical fashion, he generously tipped the tow truck driver for rescuing him from an embarrassing situation.

The next morning Bill headed off again, this time headed to Phoenix. But before he got there, a policeman pulled him over for weaving. Noting the empty wine bottles (and some full ones on ice), the officer booked Bill and threw him in jail.

After his release the next morning, Bill took off for Scottsdale, this time in a taxi. It was in Scottsdale that his brother, Jack, and longtime business associates John Saeman, Tom Marinkovich, and Tylor Johnson eventually found Bill in a hotel room, drunk and disoriented. Clearly, Bill was no longer in control of his drinking; the bottle had mastered him. But those who loved him gave him hope that he could recover.

The next day, Bill and his friends left for the Betty Ford Center. "I made up my mind that I had too many things left undone in my life to let alcohol get the best of me," Bill recounted later.

If he thought jail was humbling, rehab put him on his knees, literally. He scrubbed toilets and mopped floors alongside fellow patients, and he bared his soul in group therapy. He learned to say, "I'm an alcoholic" and dig to the roots of his addiction. No doubt Bill's upbringing

> *bill daniels*
>
> I enjoy giving people a second chance. I'm a recovering alcoholic, so know a little about that.

BETTY FORD

Dear Bill —
Thank you for being such a
thoughtful and special friend.
I just wish we could see more
of you and Jerry agrees with
me. Some day maybe we
can get you for dinner (a
quiet one.) Please be good to
yourself — We love you —
Betty

had predisposed him to addiction. His father was an alcoholic, and his sister Bobette had a drinking problem that she later overcame. Bill was determined to openly address and conquer his own alcoholism, too.

In his typically forthright manner, Bill sent an open letter to his associates, admitting that he had a problem with alcohol and was tackling it through a residential treatment program. Such a public and honest announcement was unusual in that era. If a prominent person

Bill had a long-standing friendship with Betty and President Gerald Ford.

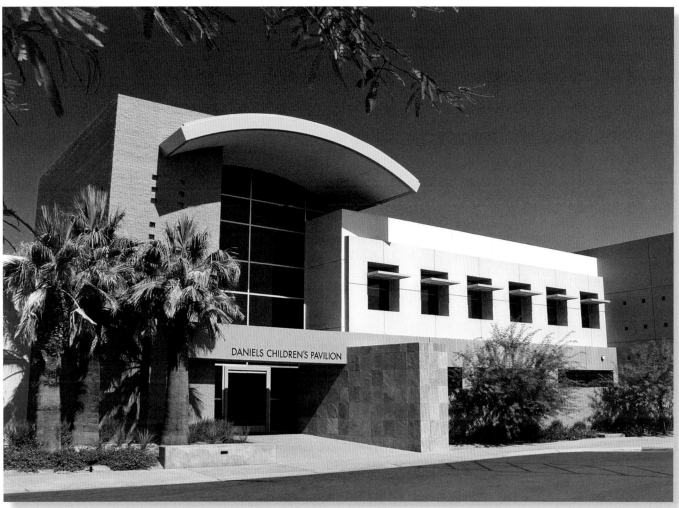

entered rehab for alcohol or substance abuse, the news was more typically kept a carefully guarded secret. It was different for Bill. He shared what he was going through in the hope that others might be helped.

When he left the Betty Ford Center that sunny day in May of 1985, Bill realized he had a second chance for a life with even greater purpose. Just three weeks after his release, he wrote Jerry Buss (co-owner of the Lakers) to explain that he went into treatment to "get my life in order not only for my personal satisfaction but to accomplish other things in my life that are left undone. I am pleased to report that I have not had a drink in 67 days. My health is exceptionally good for the way I have abused myself, and I am extremely optimistic about the future."

Bill had good reason to be. Not only did he rush headlong into some of the most creative and profitable business dealings of his career — including the launch of his regional sports network, Prime Ticket — but he became more generous and attentive to the needs of others than ever before.

The initial planning for Bill's commercial bank for kids, Young Americans Bank, began in 1985. He also entered talks with the University of Denver's College of Business to provide significant financial support. (The school was later named the Daniels College of Business in his honor.)

Bill embraced sobriety, went to Alcoholics Anonymous meetings regularly, and talked openly about

---

When he funded the construction of a children's pavilion shortly before his death in 2000, Bill became one of the top three donors in the history of the Betty Ford Center.

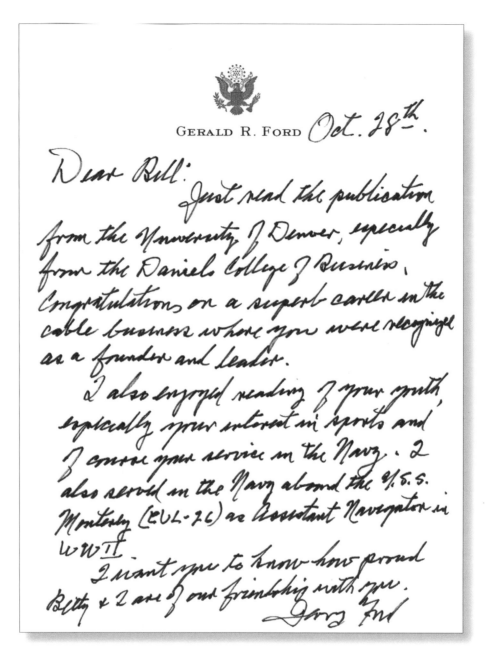

GERALD R. FORD Oct. 28th.

Dear Bill:

Just read the publication from the University of Denver, especially from the Daniels College of Business. Congratulations on a superb career in the cable business where you were recognized as a founder and leader.

I also enjoyed reading of your youth, especially your interest in sports and I envoke your service in the Navy. I also served in the Navy aboard the U.S.S. Monterey (CVL-26) as Assistant Navigator in WWII.

I want you to know how proud Betty & I are of our friendship with you.

Jerry Ford

his ongoing recovery. Far from embarrassed about his failures, Bill saw them as opportunities to teach others.

As 1985 was coming to a close, Bill wrote to a friend, reflecting on how far he had come. "January 2 will be nine months since I've had a drink," said Bill. "Isn't it strange, my business has improved tremendously since I have been sober, and I think God has something to do with that. In fact, God probably has a lot to do with it. Since I left Betty Ford Center, I have been responsible for having four of my friends go there, too. They graduated and are all doing

extremely well. I don't think I could have done it on any other basis than 'one day at a time,' simply saying I am not going to have a drink today. There are times when I am dying to have a drink, but I am pleased that the span between those times is increasing rapidly."

For the rest of his life, Bill encouraged and paid for many individuals to receive treatment for alcoholism, substance abuse, or both. Even strangers received help from Bill if he knew they were serious about getting sober. "I enjoy giving people a second chance," Bill once

A letter from President Gerald Ford to Bill.

wrote, "and I'm a recovering alcoholic, so I know a little about that."

When Bill heard about a former employee who was in an auto accident and jailed because of drunk driving, Bill wrote:

> *Wanted you to know I bleed for you. I have been in jail on more than one occasion for DUIs, and five to eight hours in jail was enough for me . . . I hope that you have learned a lesson. Meantime, you were a damn good employee here, and I want you to know I miss you. I hope that when you are released you find your way to success. I would want you to use me as a recommendation. Being a recovering alcoholic, I understand where others may not. Having been sober for over 43 months, I can tell you it does make a difference.*

In addition to providing support for friends and colleagues in need of treatment, Bill made the Betty Ford Center a priority for his philanthropy and time. The Betty Ford Center had opened in 1982, so Bill was an early patient. His support and leadership in those formative years were of great value. When he joined the board of directors in 1988, he was the first alumnus of the Betty Ford Center to serve on the board. Though Bill had been a friend of Betty and President Gerald Ford before entering treatment, the friendship deepened and lasted the rest of Bill's life.

Commenting on the active role that Bill took in the Betty Ford Center — and encouraging others who had problems similar to his — Betty Ford once reflected, "I think that recovery to Bill was a very, very valuable part of his life, just as it is to all of us. He took to it well. I don't know how many people he sat down and talked to and said, 'You know what you need to do. You need to go get help.' And he would send them to us. It was important to him to use his money to advance those who were less fortunate. That's such a beautiful part of a person's life, to be able to help somebody else."

Bill also generously supported the Betty Ford Center financially. In December of 1985, Bill wrote to six staff members who had helped him. "I have been told by the administrators at the Betty Ford Center that I am not allowed to send a Christmas gift to any one of you. In lieu of a gift to each of you, I have contributed to a fund at the Betty Ford Center in your names." He continued, "I am happy enjoying a sober life. I know it gratifies you to hear that, but I have got to tell you that you have no idea how it gratifies me."

Another large gift Bill made to the Betty Ford Center funded the construction of a meditation space. One thing Bill had missed while in rehab was a place where he could go for quiet reflection and prayer, and he rightly guessed he wasn't the only patient who needed that.

When he funded the construction of a children's pavilion shortly before his death in 2000, Bill became one of the top three donors in the history of the Betty Ford Center. When the pavilion was completed in 2002, it was named the Daniels Children's Pavilion. The facility houses programs where children of people in recovery learn that their parents' addiction is a disease, that healing is possible, and they are not to blame. The pavilion also has a fitness center, kitchen and dining room, and administrative offices.

Bill Daniels lived another 15 years after his treatment, and he remained humbled by the experience. He said more than once, "If you're gonna gamble, gamble on somebody who needs a second chance." Bill was given a second chance, and he made the most of it. He intended to keep giving second chances to others long after he was gone.

Putting Bill's Wishes into Practice

Bill's first-hand experience with the care and treatment of alcoholism resulted in clear direction to the Daniels Fund.

Bill wanted to support programs that provide direct and effective rehabilitation treatment to people suffering

NO ONE EVER THINKS THEY'LL WAKE UP HERE. METH WILL CHANGE THAT.

COLORADO METH PROJECT

METH
NOT even once.

ColoradoMethProject.org

COURTESY OF COLORADO METH PROJECT

from alcoholism and/or substance abuse. He also recognized that he was fortunate to be able to afford the travel expenses and costs of inpatient treatment, and he didn't want budget constraints to prevent anyone else from seeking help. With this in mind, the Daniels Fund supports outpatient and residential treatment services with a focus on access and affordability.

Looking back on Bill's DUI arrests and emotional suffering before he sought treatment, the Daniels Fund prioritizes services that provide for early identification and intervention. Bill did not want alcoholism or substance abuse to cause people to waste another day of their lives in jail, on the streets, or in distress when help was available.

Much of the overall focus for Bill's foundation is to help young people succeed. Few things are more likely to derail a young person from a positive future than alcohol and drugs. Therefore, the Daniels Fund supports prevention, especially programs directed toward youth.

Finally, Bill knew that getting sober was only the first step in recovery. Success means staying sober while pursuing new opportunities for learning, working, and helping others. Bill knew the value that support groups offer to a person trying to get through the day without a drink. He also recognized that people face obstacles after rehab that can limit their opportunities.

Given these perspectives, the Daniels Fund is committed to supportive services and after-care facilities that help people make the most of their lives. Access and affordability of such services were important to Bill and are important to the Daniels Fund.

The Daniels Fund supports programs that focus on the prevention of alcoholism and substance abuse, especially among youth.

CHAPTER SIXTEEN

AMATEUR SPORTS

If you didn't mow the lawn, you didn't get your allowance. You told a lie and got grounded for a week. If you weren't a team player, you sat on the bench. It's called discipline. And it's not only an important part of growing up. It's an important part of your entire life.

~ Bill Daniels

The Daniels Fund supports programs that expand opportunities for participation in quality youth sports programs that foster sportsmanship, confidence, discipline, and teamwork. Additionally, support is provided for programs that expand opportunities for national and international amateur sports competition.

Bill's Story

When Bob Daniels put his son Bill on a bus to Roswell, New Mexico, he was hoping for a miracle. It was 1937, and Bill was a scrappy 17-year-old who never backed down from a fight. It could have been that the young Bill needed more activity to keep him occupied than the small town of Hobbs, New Mexico, could provide. But at the time, Bob was more than a little concerned that his son was headed down the wrong path. With any luck, military school would put him on the right one.

The military drills, rigid discipline, and challenging coursework provided by New Mexico Military Institute (NMMI) taught Bill self-control and gave him respect for authority. But it was his participation in sports that showed Bill who he could become.

Bill (#15 in the middle), led his NMMI basketball team to an undefeated season.

COLT FOOTBALL

Back Row: Capt. Storm, Yoakum, Okerstrom, Watson, Reis, Bradley, Hueter, Kelly, Ramsden, Daniels, Rihl, Edwards, Alcour, Wolfe, Sanderson

Front Row: Fowler, Park, Rollie, Hagerty, Allen, Dean, Walker, Cook, McPhail

COLT BASKETBALL

Capt. Storm, Porter, Katz, Daniels, Dunn, Hall, Johnson, Walker, Fowler, Dufek, Corliss, Sheridan, Hueter

At NMMI, Bill played on the basketball and football teams (pictured here), as well as the baseball and boxing teams.

When Bill enrolled at NMMI as a high school junior, he had no history of playing organized sports. He was a full head shorter than most of the other guys on campus and, though he was strong, he wasn't sure he could compete. Instead, he applied to be manager of the football team. The football coach, Clark Storm, put his arm around Bill and said, "Son, we don't need a manager. We need players!"

Bill was Coach Storm's starting quarterback for the next two years and also played linebacker. He made All-State in both positions. Sixty years later, Bill remembered Coach Storm as "a real sweetheart who passed along his high principles."

NMMI's other coach, Colonel L. T. "Babe" Godfrey, took one look at Bill Daniels and recruited him for the baseball, basketball, and boxing teams as well. Bill lettered in football and basketball his first year. As a senior, he led the basketball team to an undefeated season.

Coach Godfrey is credited with giving Bill the nickname "Jeep," which his NMMI friends called him the rest of his life. The coach, admiring Bill's tenacity, compared him to a US Army Jeep: "an indestructible mini-tank that was small, sturdy, tough, and, being four-wheel driven, could go anywhere." Bill was always ready to play a full game of football or basketball and, according to the coach, was "always good for three rounds in the Golden Gloves — unless, to the discomfiture of his opponent, it went for fewer rounds."

In later life, Bill credited his coaches for embedding in him the principles that led to his future success, including discipline, teamwork, drive, fair play, and commitment. Of Coach Godfrey, Bill said, "He's the guy I probably admire most, next to my dad. He has been a magnificent mentor to me, and I have tried to follow his principles: hustle, hard work, don't give up, you're a small guy — so what? Size doesn't mean anything. He taught me patriotism — to love my nation, love my country, and love my fellow man. He was just a magnificent man." Coach Godfrey lived into his nineties, and Bill stayed in

touch with him as long as he lived. Bill visited him twice a year to "let him know how grateful I am."

After completing high school at NMMI in 1939, Bill stayed on there for two years of junior college. He refined his boxing skills as an amateur welterweight fighter and had 42 fights. He became a New Mexico Golden Gloves champion and hung up his boxing gloves only after breaking his hand in what was to be his last fight.

Amateur sports became one of Bill's lifelong passions. Indeed, the first television show Bill ever saw — a discovery that changed the course of his life — was *Wednesday Night Fights*, which was broadcast live from New York City.

"Boxing has been my favorite sport for a long time," he wrote to a friend near the end of his life. "I fought as an amateur, and I feel there are ways we can uplift the image of boxing to the American public."

Bill knew that amateur sports could turn lives around, as it had his. After he settled in Denver in the 1960s, he organized the Denver Boxing Club, which reached out to dozens of youth. Said Bill, "It occurred to me that boxing had done a lot for me and that it would be a good way to get a bunch of kids off the streets and involved in something that would build character and teach self-sufficiency."

In 1969 Bill financed an amateur boxing team called the Denver Rocks, which offered fighters of every weight class an opportunity to get in the ring and test their skills. The fighters were trained by a veteran boxer and fought at the Denver Coliseum.

Bill always kept his eyes open for young athletes who needed a leg up. He spoke at parole boards on behalf of prison inmates with boxing skills, and he brought four young fighters from an impoverished New York City neighborhood to fight in Denver (for which Bill was awarded the New York City Golden Gloves trophy).

"More club owners in sports should be on the lookout for talent among the downtrodden and sometimes hopeless people," Bill once told a reporter. "They are hungry. They have a desire, a competitive heart."

Boxing wasn't the only amateur sport that caught Bill's attention. Interestingly, he found a friend and a new opportunity in the world of competitive figure skating.

When Scott Hamilton won the men's figure skating Olympic gold medal at the 1984 Games, Bill arranged a victory parade for him in Denver. The two became friends, and Bill helped sponsor Scott's career.

In 1997, when Scott was going through chemotherapy for cancer, Bill insisted he use Bill's jet to fly home from his treatments at a distant hospital. It was Bill's thoughtfulness that inspired Scott to become a philanthropist and start a cancer fund. "I want to invest in something that will continue to give and give long after I am gone," said Scott. "I learned a lot from Bill. The people I love and respect the most are the ones that have taken what they have been given and turned it into

Coach "Babe" Godfrey (right) was Bill's mentor and friend, and they stayed in close contact throughout their lives.

something beyond success. Bill was one of the greatest examples of that."

In another instance, Bill was sympathetic when he learned that local figure skater Allyson Fenlon needed help covering her training costs. Bill sent a check to Allyson's father with a letter that said, "Delighted I can help. I admire kids who have the dedication to compete in sports."

Bill helped other athletes by encouraging their careers after sports. In a letter to the dean of the University of Denver College of Law, Bill recommended college senior Bryan Pattison for admittance to the law school. He used Bryan's integrity on the high school football field as evidence of his qualifications. "Bryan is a young man who has never met a challenge he did not attempt to conquer," wrote Bill. "When I first heard about Bryan, he was a wide receiver for the Bingham High football team in Salt Lake City, Utah. He did not possess the speed a lot of receivers had. But he always showed his true grit with his intensity on the field. Bryan became an all-region wide receiver. He was never afraid to give up his body to help a team effort and was always a team player. He was the type of player coaches love to talk about . . . He wants to succeed in life, and I know he will."

In short, Bill believed former athletes were likely to have developed many of the same principles he had learned on the field, on the court, and in the ring. And he was quick to recognize and acknowledge when an athlete in the public eye behaved with dignity and upstanding principles.

To Roger Staubach, former quarterback for the Dallas Cowboys (and a fellow NMMI alum), Bill wrote, "I keep up with your operations, and I thoroughly enjoyed it when you and your staff came by and had lunch with me in my home. Looking at athletes who really count — Michael Jordan, Wayne Gretzky, John Elway, and yourself — you all have outstanding ability but, even more so, the character that many people should have: integrity, ethics, hard work, and the love of God."

Those types of comments were typical for Bill to make, but others voiced the same sentiments about Bill himself. "People sometimes forget what an outstanding athlete Bill was, and that played into much of his career later on," reflected Bill's colleague Hank Brown. "I've often thought that the lessons he learned through athletics were fundamental to his success in business: his willingness to stick with things no matter how tough, to give a project everything he had, his commitment to fair play."

Putting Bill's Wishes into Practice

It is hardly a surprise that Bill Daniels directed his foundation to support amateur sports. Put simply, he believed that playing a sport can change the direction of a person's life. After all, he was living proof.

Participation in amateur sports developed many of the qualities Bill admired in a human being. Among those were sportsmanship and fair play, hard work and persistence, confidence and the ability to overcome limitations, and discipline and follow-through, as well as competitive drive and teamwork.

He also knew that these principles are best learned early in life so that they can be applied to school, work, relationships, and community. Bill's high school coaches made a significant difference in the man he became, and their high standards prepared him well for military service, career advancement, and leadership. Often, when Bill admired a colleague's character, he could attribute it to a background in sports.

Therefore, the Daniels Fund directs its support of amateur sports to expand and enhance opportunities for youth. Grants are made to community-based and after school youth sports programs. In addition, knowing the critical role a coach plays in communicating and fostering character development, the Daniels Fund supports efforts to ensure quality coaching and training for young athletes.

Looking beyond Bill's own early years to his lifetime of promoting amateur athletic competition, the Daniels Fund continues his efforts with support for national and international amateur sports competitions. Grant funding is also made available for local and state competitions that qualify athletes for national and international events.

Bill never wavered in his commitment to expand opportunities for athletic competition. Neither does the Daniels Fund.

TOP | *Funding for participation in quality sports programs allows young people of all ages to learn discipline, confidence, and sportsmanship.* BOTTOM | *Bill believed that the sport of boxing taught young people the importance of hard work, playing fair, and never giving up.*

CHAPTER SEVENTEEN

DISABILITIES

Everybody is important to me. We are all human beings on the face of this earth.
~ Bill Daniels

Bill with his sister Dorothy, who was developmentally disabled.

The Daniels Fund supports programs that assist individuals with physical and developmental disabilities and their families in achieving and maintaining independence and quality of life. This is achieved by funding supportive services for those dealing with developmental disabilities and by making equipment available to those with physical disabilities.

Bill's Story

The piano music stopped Bill in his tracks. He had walked into a mall in La Jolla, California, to do a little shopping, and he'd intended to get in and get out. But now he couldn't get past the atrium. Sunlight streamed down onto a piano player who was making such beautiful music that Bill forgot he was in a hurry.

VALUE people FOR
WHAT THEY CAN DO,
NOT FOR WHAT THEY CAN'T.

He marveled not only at the man's talent but also at his ability to play so well when he was obviously blind.

Bill stayed and listened for half an hour, tipped the piano player generously, and then continued his shopping expedition. The music put him in such a good mood that he spent more than he'd planned and called some friends later to encourage them to visit the mall to hear the musician. When they heard the man play, they agreed with Bill that he was exceptional.

Though Bill never spoke with the man, he somehow learned that the pianist's name was Jimmy Carroll. Bill guessed Jimmy was 65, just a little older than Bill was at the time. Bill also discovered that Jimmy earned no money at the mall other than tips and that the manager thought Jimmy was a nuisance and was trying to get rid of him.

This knowledge was too much for Bill's big heart and business sensibilities. Within days, he was dictating a letter to the manager, chastising him for wanting to get rid of someone who had triumphed over blindness and whose talents had drawn people to the mall and into its stores. Who knows if anything came of that 1981 letter? But Bill felt compelled to send it, and advocate for the musician. The fact that Jimmy Carroll was blind was secondary to the fact that he was hugely talented, but underappreciated and grossly undercompensated.

This story speaks to Bill's overall perspective on people with disabilities as much as it represents his desire to help others when he could. Bill clearly felt that people were people first, and they should be valued for what they *could do*, not for what they *couldn't*. At the same time, Bill realized that life was not always fair.

It was a lesson he learned early, growing up with his sister Dorothy, who was developmentally disabled. She was one year older than Bill, but he quickly matured past her abilities. Given the medical knowledge of the 1920s and 1930s, the exact diagnosis of Dorothy's condition is unclear today, but her mental function never developed beyond that of a 12-year-old. No one expected she would live past the age of 20.

The news might have been devastating to the Daniels family, but the attitude of acceptance and devotion that Bill's parents modeled had a lasting impact on Bill. At a time when society often institutionalized children with disabilities, Dorothy grew up at home with her loving family around her. She was encouraged to be involved in activities and participate however she was able.

Dorothy lived into her sixties — far outliving all projections — thanks mostly to the loving care of her mother, Adele. Once Bill's father died and the other Daniels children left home, Adele took on the sole responsibility for her daughter, always making it crystal clear how she wanted others to treat Dorothy.

"They expected all of us to treat her as a normal part of our family, and we loved her," reflected Bill's niece Diane Denish about her Aunt Dotty. "She had a memory like an elephant — she never forgot anything — and she adored her brother Bill like no other person on earth." The family eventually made the tough decision to move Dorothy to a nearby complete care facility when Adele became unable to provide the level of care she knew her daughter required and deserved.

During times when he was away from Hobbs and his family there, Bill kept in touch with his sister through thoughtful letters. He wrote in a simplified style, sometimes referring to himself in the third person to help her understand. Dorothy died at the age of 67, one year before Adele passed away. Bill honored his sister with ongoing financial support to the facility that

Bill Daniels
CHAIRMAN

August 6, 1985

Dotty sweetheart,

Just a note to say "Hi". Bill has been in California for 3½ weeks and got back to Denver on Sunday night. Talked to Jack today and to Mother. They both tell me you are getting along fine. I understand you are helping the nurses and other people, and that is very nice, Dotty. You can make a big contribution by helping other people and being nice like you have always been.

I am very busy right now, but as soon as I can I want to come by and surprise you.

In the meantime, Bill loves you very much. Enclosed is a little walking around money for you to enjoy.

I love you,

Bill

2930 East Third Avenue
P.O. Box 6008
Denver, Colorado 80206-0008
303 321-7550

During times when he was away from Hobbs and his family there, Bill kept in touch with his sister Dorothy through thoughtful letters.

had provided compassionate care for her as well as with donations to other organizations.

Growing up with a disabled family member clearly enhanced Bill's sensitivity to the limitations people face, and those who were able to overcome their limitations impressed him.

Making the best of life was Bill's motto when he began to acknowledge his own disability — severe hearing loss — around age 70. Largely thanks to the deafening noise levels he experienced during his fighter-pilot days in the 1940s and 1950s, the function in one ear was reduced to 30 percent. Then on New Year's Day in 1992, Bill woke to discover he had total hearing loss in his other ear.

As time went on, Bill found it difficult and deeply embarrassing to participate at social events. It was almost impossible for him to hear in large gatherings, and even quiet, one-on-one conversations became increasingly challenging. He stopped giving speeches, going out with friends, and traveling for pleasure. The isolation of being hearing-impaired hit home, and Bill experienced the social and psychological tolls of a disability.

Still, it took a while for Bill to accept his hearing loss, and took still longer for him to seek the help of specialists and explore amplification technologies. His denial of his worsening situation — coupled by his delay in seeking treatment — he later regretted. Sadly, Bill's hearing never significantly improved.

When Bill's great-nephew was experiencing hearing problems, Bill encouraged him to address them as soon as possible. "As you are well aware, my hearing has degenerated in the last year, primarily because I did not do anything about it early in life," Bill told him in a letter. "I urge you to find an ear specialist in Albuquerque. Find out who is the best and have him give you an examination . . . I have been told by the finest ear specialist that if I'd paid attention to my problem in the early stages it would not have gotten to this point today. Forget vanity. Get with it. Do it for Uncle Bill. Mostly, do it for yourself."

Bill was 73 when he wrote to his old Navy buddy and fellow pilot Donal "Broe" Broesamle that he was "really struggling" with the severe hearing loss. "I can't even visit with anybody if there's background noise. Doctors say part of it is from fighter-pilot days that you and I know about. Anyway, if that is the worst thing that happens to me, I won't complain. I have been a lucky guy."

Putting Bill's Wishes into Practice

Given his personal experiences with his sister's disability and with his own physical impairment in later life, it is no surprise that Bill Daniels wanted to fund services for people with disabilities.

Bill witnessed firsthand how his mother's care at home gave Dorothy a better quality of life. Yet he also understood the stress placed on the caregivers of those with special needs. Thus, the Daniels Fund supports programs that enable in-home care of people with developmental disabilities, provide family / caregiver training, and offer respite care.

The Grants Program is also motivated by the people who inspired Bill as they overcame disabilities to live their lives as independently as possible. Therefore, funding is available for early identification of developmental disabilities, intervention programs, and vocational programs that will give individuals every chance of successful, independent futures.

Bill's own hearing loss helped him understand the challenges associated with having a physical disability. He particularly noted the value of equipment to overcome these challenges.

Mobility and rehabilitative equipment is costly, often prohibitively so. Life-altering equipment may not be an option for the uninsured or the under-insured. The Daniels Fund, therefore, provides funding for programs that make it easier for individuals with physical disabilities to purchase or borrow relevant equipment. These programs may also refurbish and repair equipment, set up equipment loan banks, provide support for users, and build awareness of available programs and resources.

TOP | *The Daniels Fund supports programs that provide equipment allowing maximum independence for people with disabilities.*
BOTTOM | *People with hearing loss who need hearing aids or other equipment may be eligible for assistance from the Daniels Fund.*

CHAPTER EIGHTEEN

EARLY CHILDHOOD EDUCATION

Quality education for all should be our goal.
~ Bill Daniels

The Daniels Fund supports programs that improve the quality of the early childhood education system to ensure school readiness by focusing on teacher / leadership quality, facility quality, and parental involvement.

Bill's Story

In the last year of his life, Bill Daniels took time to write to the grandson of his friend *Cablevision Magazine* publisher, Bill McGorry. The whole point of the letter to young Will was to encourage him to do his best in school.

"Will, you are my pal and I want to make sure that you take advantage of the future out there in front of you, for your entire lifetime," Bill wrote. "Admission to a good college or university requires good grades. So, your old pal, Bill, wants you to know that the better your grades are every year, the better the university you will enter."

It was not unusual for Bill to write a child directly, or to focus on that child's education. He often reminded children of the importance of doing well in school so

Bill is pictured with the son of a business associate during a family outing.

January 27, 2000

Dear Pam and Will,

I thank both of you for your nice letter. Pam, nice to hear from you and my little buddy, Will. At Will's age, he will not absorb the value of a college education, but he will every year he gets older. He will understand how important it is to have young people go to college.

Will, you are my pal and I want to make sure that you take advantage of the future out there in front of you, for your entire lifetime. Admission to a good college or university requires good grades. So, your old pal, Bill, wants you to know that the better your grades are every year, the better the university you will enter. I am sure your Grandpa will want to talk you into St. John's, which is good enough for me if it's good enough for you, your Mom, and Grandpa.

One of these days I hope to see you again, Will. I know you are growing like a weed and I know the love and affection your Grandpa has for you, as well as the rest of your family. So be a good guy and make all your family proud.

Pam, again, I'm thankful for your note and thankful to know your Father, who happens to be one of the finest guys I have ever known.

Fondly,

Bill

Bill Daniels

BD/sg

5720 EL CAMINO REAL
CARLSBAD, CALIFORNIA 92008
619/438-7721

Always quick to stress the importance of good grades, Bill wrote this letter to the grandson of one of his colleagues, encouraging him to do well in school.

At the same time, Bill encouraged young people by communicating high expectations to their parents. Many of his colleagues were parents, and he saw the difference that good parenting can make in raising upstanding, hard-working young people. Bill often complimented his closest associates about the wonderful job they were doing raising their children. And Bill enjoyed it when his associates bragged to him about their children's achievements. Bill often congratulated the children directly. To one youngster he wrote:

Last week your mother showed me your report card, and I can't believe it happened again. I am getting used to seeing you get all As! You would be amazed how few students are able to continue to do so. You will realize as you grow older how important it is to make excellent grades, whatever grade and whatever school you are in, and to continue to have the great attitude you have about everything you undertake. I am extremely proud of you, dear.

Bill understood that educational expectations for youth in modern society are much different than when he was growing up. When Bill was young, it was rare for mothers to work outside the home. Neighborhoods were safe havens for children, who could roam freely and seek adventure and fun in creative, independent ways. Though Bill rarely talked about his own early schooling, it seems clear that he learned a great deal at home from his parents, and from exploring and playing with siblings and friends.

Decades later, as he was setting up his foundation, times had changed. Bill described the need for early childhood education that provides a "healthy, safe, nurturing, and stimulating environment." Through his friendships with parents and their children, he realized that many families counted on early childhood programs to provide necessary childcare as well as a child's first

bill daniels

WE NEED EARLY CHILDHOOD EDUCATION THAT PROVIDES A HEALTHY, SAFE, NURTURING, & STIMULATING ENVIRONMENT.

that they could broaden their options for the future. Bill wanted their learning experiences to foster good values and unlimited opportunity.

Bill was charmed by the child of an associate.

educational opportunities outside the home. He also knew how important parents are to their children's early and long-term success. Bill wanted to be sure that early learning experiences put children on a successful path from the start.

Putting Bill's Wishes into Practice

The Daniels Fund focuses on the total system of early childhood education. Because Bill Daniels strived for quality in every aspect of his life and work, funding in this area focuses on teacher/leadership quality and facility quality for early childhood programs. The Daniels Fund also seeks to enhance parental involvement in early childhood education through information and outreach programs to parents.

TOP PHOTOS | *Parental involvement combined with great teachers and facilities help ensure school readiness for kids.* BOTTOM | *Bill's goal in establishing the Early Childhood Education funding area was to provide excellent educational opportunities for kids preparing to enter school.*

CHAPTER NINETEEN

K-12 EDUCATION REFORM

I am a great believer in the basic reading, writing, and arithmetic. Add to that good manners, ethics, and integrity. With that, our young people will do well.

~ Bill Daniels

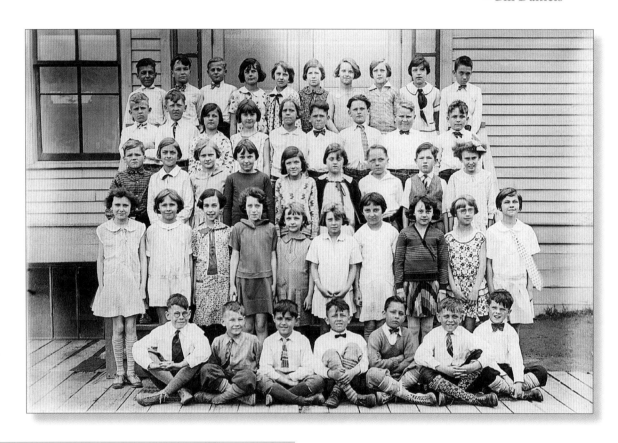

The Daniels Fund supports programs that improve the quality of the K-12 educational system to ensure increased student achievement by focusing on reform and school choice, parental engagement, and teacher/ leadership quality.

Bill's Story

During parents' night at the school that one of his stepchildren was attending, Bill stood in the back of the room with his arms crossed as he listened intently to the teacher's presentation. The longer he listened, the more impatient he became. *How in the world is this particular material relevant?* Bill wondered.

After a few minutes, he couldn't contain himself any longer. He raised his hand, and the teacher called on him. "I am Bill Daniels, and I just want to know what the hell this will do for people in the real world? It will have *no relevance.*"

The teacher maintained her composure and did her best to explain how her course could help with language development and wider thinking. Her answers were unconvincing to Bill.

Bill is sitting second from the right on the front row in this photo taken in 1930 of his fourth-grade class.

The next day, the teacher went on teaching what she thought was important, but Bill had made his point. He wanted education to be *relevant*. He wanted schools to provide knowledge and expertise that would help prepare young people to be successful in life. And he wanted schools to teach the same kind of practical skills, such as discipline and etiquette, that he had learned at the New Mexico Military Institute.

Over the next few years, Bill became increasingly committed to making positive changes where he could, often serving as a guest lecturer, and frequently making donations to schools. More often than not, he was stunned and dismayed by the wide disparity between the skills businesses needed their employees to possess and the skills educational systems were providing.

"I cannot describe to you the frustration that exists for an entrepreneur dealing with the academic community," Bill lamented in a 1993 letter to a colleague. "It takes them forever to get anything done . . . And you can't fire the incompetents without the most serious offense."

Late in 1993, he wrote how disheartened he was to read about a national poll that found 84 percent of people over 60 felt they received a better education in their youth than children at the time were getting. As proud as he was of his country, he worried that inadequate education was going to diminish the nation's global competitiveness.

Bill was intrigued by efforts to reform public education through vouchers and charter schools. These innovations were just beginning to gain momentum in the early 1990s, and Bill was already writing about them to friends. He believed that competition enabled by parental choice would force schools to improve.

"I do like the school voucher system program like Michigan just voted in which says that if anyone wants to send their child to a private school, the government will pay $2,500 of the tuition per year via voucher," wrote Bill. "This gives everyone the true choice in where to send their children to school."

In November 1998, Bill supported an amendment to the state constitution in Colorado that would provide an income tax credit to the parents or guardians of children

Bill, talking to a young man in his office, took every opportunity he could to guide and encourage young people.

December 27, 1990

Mr. Bo Peretto
17998 E. Prentice Place
Aurora, CO 80015

Dear Bo,

Thank you for your thank you note, which I would like to quote to you. You said "I thank you for starting my new business." That isn't the way it is, Bo. It is <u>our</u> new business until such time as you repay the $50.00 to the Young Americans Bank.

I appreciate your sending me your report card, which I think you will agree leaves room for improvement. I would like to see all "H" for high quality. I know you are capable. No more of this "satisfactory" business.

The agreement that you sent to me between the two of us is satisfactory. I am grateful for your prompt response.

Good luck,

Your pal, Bill

5720 EL CAMINO REAL
CARLSBAD, CALIFORNIA 92008
619/438-7721

One of Bill's letters to a young man, encouraging him to strive for good grades and high quality.

February 21, 1996

Ms. Susan Poutre
Assistant Principal
Merrill Middle School
1551 South Monroe Street
Denver, CO 80210

Dear Ms. Poutre,

Without your vision, enthusiasm, patience, instruction, and encouragement, our world speed record attempt may have been a bust. Your students' beautiful pictures and warm wishes — the most precious cargo the crew has ever carried (except maybe me) — became an inspiration. This motivated the pilots to race to each destination just to see the next group of bright faces and colorful greetings.

I can't tell you how proud I am to know it was my plane that delivered the return greetings to your kids at Wednesday's ceremony. What a well-behaved group! And I was absolutely astounded by their poise at the podium.

The way Merrill's students handled themselves is a real tribute to the quality education they are receiving. I commend you and your group, and I thank you for a job well done.

Fondly,

Bill Daniels

BD:lar

5720 EL CAMINO REAL
CARLSBAD, CALIFORNIA 92008
619/438-7721

in public, non-public, or home-based education programs. He hoped Colorado's example would lead the other 49 states to follow suit. Although the amendment was defeated, Bill continued to believe in the potential of applying free enterprise principles, like choice and competition, to the educational system.

He specifically identified support for charter schools when setting up the Daniels Fund. His hope was that if schools were freed of constraints — such as teachers' unions and tenure, imposed curricula, and rigid schedules — they would have the flexibility to create schools of excellence.

Of course, Bill was quick to praise traditional schools and teachers when they taught the values he felt were important, such as self-confidence, respect, and caring for others. For example, in 1996 Bill sponsored a round-the-world flight to set a new speed record for a business jet. In conjunction with the flight, students at Denver's

Bill thanked Merrill Middle School students for their enthusiasm for the world speed record attempt.

Merrill Middle School produced drawings and letters to be delivered to school children greeting the plane at each refueling stop along the route.

Bill was thrilled by this project and wrote to the school's assistant principal after the successful flight to tell her so. "Without your vision, enthusiasm, instruction, and encouragement, our world speed record attempt may have been a bust," he wrote. "Your students' beautiful pictures and warm wishes — the most precious cargo the crew has ever carried (except maybe me) — became an inspiration. This motivated the pilots to race to each destination."

There was a ceremony after the flight that included students from Merrill. "I was absolutely astounded by their poise at the podium," Bill wrote. "The way Merrill's students handled themselves is a real tribute to the quality education they are receiving. I commend you and your group, and I thank you for a job well done."

Putting Bill's Wishes into Practice

Bill Daniels was explicit in his desire to improve K-12 public and private educational systems through strategies that included charter schools and voucher programs. He believed such alternatives would foster excellent schools and student achievement through competition and choice.

Therefore, the Daniels Fund provides assistance to plan, start, and operate charter schools as well as to ensure high-quality teachers and leaders in these schools. Grants are also made for tuition assistance (voucher) programs that are clearly in keeping with Bill's belief in the need to force the education system to respond to the demands of a free market. The Daniels Fund also supports projects that challenge public and private schools to operate more like businesses. The Daniels Fund supports Bill's convictions that great improvements in education can be made by removing barriers to reform and that compensation should be based on results, not tenure.

Finally, Bill understood that parents need to be informed consumers so they will take an active role in propelling schools toward excellence. Therefore, the Daniels Fund supports parental engagement through education, resources, and parental advocacy.

TOP | *In conjunction with the world speed record flight, students at Denver's Merrill Middle School produced drawings and letters to be delivered to school children greeting the plane at each refueling stop along the route.* BOTTOM | *Encouraging students to be active and engaged in the classroom ensures increased student achievement.*

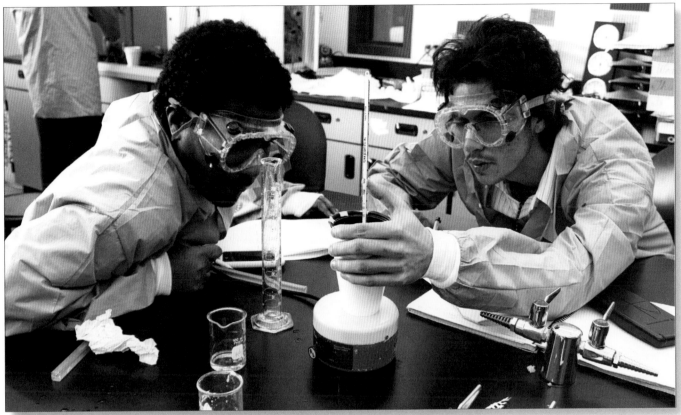

COURTESY OF DENVER SCHOOL OF SCIENCE AND TECHNOLOGY

COURTESY OF BYRNE URBAN SCHOLARS

TOP | *Ensuring that all students have access to quality educational programs is a primary goal of the K-12 Education Reform funding area for the Daniels Fund.* BOTTOM | *Helping students graduate from high school and move on to college or other productive career paths is also a goal of the Daniels Fund.*

ETHICS AND INTEGRITY IN EDUCATION

I'm hopeful that my investment in ethics education will bear fruit in the decades ahead so that young people don't just look toward personal gain as their chief objective in life.

~ Bill Daniels

The Daniels Fund supports programs that improve the quality of the ethics curriculum in education to foster principle-based leadership from kindergarten through college.

Bill's Story

Bill was alone in a Salt Lake City hotel room when he was forced to come to terms with a devastating reality. It was December of 1975, and his American Basketball Association (ABA) team, the Utah Stars, was bankrupt. His bank had just told him, "You can't go any further," and had shut down his credit. With no money to pay his players and staff, Bill watched the Stars leave the court for the last time as a team.

Bill stood at the window, eight floors up, looking over the city he felt he had failed. He put his head in his hands and cried. He had invested $5 million in this venture, but it wasn't the money that upset him. It was all the people he was going to hurt: the players and coaches who were out of a job; the vendors at the arena whose businesses were

When the University of Denver renamed the business school the Daniels College of Business, Bill spoke at the ceremony.

suddenly without customers; the season ticket holders who were now holding worthless passes; the thousands of fans who loved their winning basketball team.

The Utah Stars' financial situation off the court was in stark contrast to their performance on the court. They were champions. When Bill bought the team and moved it from Los Angeles to Salt Lake City in 1970, the Stars set an ABA attendance record and won the 1971 ABA championship. Bill was thrilled to watch 13,000 screaming fans cheer the team to victory in Game 7 at the Salt Palace. The Stars played in the division finals the next two years and returned once again in 1974.

None of that seemed to matter, now that the money had run out. He pulled himself together, and called his lawyer to talk about next steps. "I am heartbroken," Bill confessed. Reaching deep for a moment of badly needed humor, Bill joked, "I'm gonna jump out of this window."

Without missing a beat, Bill's attorney replied, "Bill, with the luck you're having, you'd live."

Bill didn't jump that day, but living through the whole bankruptcy process left him shattered by feelings of shame and failure. Even though his legal and financial obligations were discharged, it was of no consolation to Bill. He was devastated.

However, he never forgot the people he let down, and he was driven to do right by them, not because it was required by law, but for himself. He declared that someday he would be back to repay his debts.

Five years later, after rebuilding his financial strength, he returned to Salt Lake City and kept his word by repaying his creditors, season ticket holders, vendors, and players. But he didn't just repay the principal. He also added eight percent interest per year for each of the five years. It personally cost Bill more than $750,000 to make this unprecedented gesture. As for the people and businesses that Bill could not locate through searches and full-page newspaper ads, he donated their share to the City of Salt Lake.

Many years later, Bill reflected on his actions when he addressed a group of Casper College business students. "Boy, I suffered when the Stars went bankrupt. I had no legal obligation to do what I did, but it bugged my conscience," he told them. "I suffered when the team folded, and I had to look myself in the mirror every morning and face head-on what had happened."

There was never a question in Bill's mind that he would repay his debts. And doing so had a lasting impact. As Bill told the students at Casper, "Even today I meet people who say, 'Aren't you the guy who paid that money back to those basketball fans in Salt Lake City all those years ago?'"

Before continuing with his story, Bill paused to survey the students packing the room. "It shows you how in the long term, having ethics and integrity pays off," he said. People in Utah recognized Bill's extraordinary gesture, and later commemorated his honorable actions by making him the first inductee to the Utah Sports Legends Hall of Fame.

Building a reputation of integrity was a lifelong pursuit for Bill. In 1952 he opened a small insurance agency in Casper, Wyoming, and struggled to make it over the next three years. Then in 1955, one of the insurance companies he represented went broke, leaving the policyholders high and dry. Bill stepped in for his client, feeling that *he* had represented the terms and *his* integrity was at stake. As he explained:

Two weeks after the bankruptcy, Burlington Railroad sued one of my clients — to whom I had sold a liability policy — for $12,500. A judgment was entered against my client for $11,000. I made a deal with Burlington Railroad to pay this judgment off at $500 per month, over a 22-month period. I did not have to do this, but I had a strong conviction that I owed this to my insured who had placed his faith in my handling of his insurance business. During this time, the $500 payment was more than I was making per month. I managed, however, through borrowing and juggling of finances, to do this.

In all aspects of his life, Bill was committed to doing the right thing. "I want to leave the face of the earth with a good reputation," he said. "When I'm gone, I don't ever want anyone to say that Bill Daniels stiffed them."

His integrity was not just about keeping promises, however. It also meant being honest in all circumstances and disclosing all potential conflicts of interest. When Bill was the second president of the National Community Television Association (NCTA) in 1956, he saw there were great opportunities for brokering deals between cable companies. "I had people calling me, saying they either wanted to buy a cable system or sell one," he remembered. "I put buyers and sellers together, but I would not take a fee, because in my view I was part of the national trade association. I didn't think it was proper." Brokering deals would become a huge part of his business career, but he didn't start that business until after his tenure as NCTA president was over.

Part of Bill's formula for success was to make sure that deals were a win-win for all parties and to truly care about the people who would be impacted by the transactions. "The numbers are often secondary," he maintained.

The commitment of Daniels & Associates to always do what was right became well known in the industry and earned Bill great respect and loyalty. "They have a real reputation for square dealing," a colleague told a reporter from *Electronic Media* in 1989. "They got to where they are today by providing good service and having integrity."

Brian Deevy, who worked with Bill for 25 years at Daniels & Associates, reflected on how that philosophy drove Bill's company as well as his life. "The quality I admired about Bill from Day 1 was his focus on integrity and ethics. He drilled it into us every chance he got, and that's the way Daniels & Associates was run," said Brian. "I could see it in every negotiation, every deal that

he did. Many of those deals were sealed by a handshake, and we never had an issue. Everything in his life was driven by that." Comments like that were high praise to Bill. "The integrity of this firm means more to me than dollars," he wrote to a friend.

The Salt Lake Tribune, Wednesday, July 9, 1980 C 3

Daniels Plans to Repay Stars' Ticket Holders

By Lex Hemphill
Tribune Sports Writer

It was "four years, seven months, and eight days ago" that Bill Daniels folded the American Basketball Association Utah Stars.

He knows the numbers. The fact that he can quote them indicates the extent to which his conscience may have been counting them since the day he left Salt Lake City.

And so Daniels returned to Salt Lake Tuesday and announced at a press conference that now he is ready to pay off all the season ticket holders of the Utah Stars in the curtailed 1975-76 season, in which the Stars played only nine of 42 home games before going under.

It is something that Daniels does not have to do. His Mountain States Sports, Inc., the corporation that operated the Stars, filed for bankruptcy four years ago, and the class action lawsuit brought against MSSI by burned season ticket holders was settled out of court two years ago.

He has no obligations, and he denies that he has any intentions of re-establishing himself business-wise either in Utah or in professional sports. The real obligation he says he's meeting is one to himself.

"I don't want to leave the face of the earth owing one dime," said Daniels, who noted he was not in financial position to make this payback gesture before now.

So Daniels, who folded the Stars on Dec. 1, 1975, has devised a plan of compensation that could personally cost him in the neighborhood of $750,000.

He plans to pay the 724 Stars' season ticket holders $346,620.77 for the 33 unplayed games of the 1975-76 season, plus interest at the rate of eight percent per year. The added interest would set the total amount of reimbursement due season ticket holders at approximatelt $460,000.

In addition, Daniels plans to recompense what he terms "the bona fide and non-contested Utah vendors and suppliers of the Stars," a group which would include local merchants who served the Stars. It is estimated that these additional payments could send the Daniels paybacks into the vicinity of $750,000.

Daniels said that letters were mailed out Tuesday to the season ticket holders and the suppliers and vendors, informing them of his intentions and including verification cards that the customers are asked to submit. In the event that ticket holders either do not respond or can't be located, Daniels said he will donate their return to an as-yet-undetermined charity in Utah.

While Daniels was instituting his repayment plan Tuesday, his local attorney, Michael Heyrend, said he was filing a document with the Third District Court, seeking "appropriate relief" from Daniels' obligation to pay off the settlement reached in the class action suit that was brought against him back on Dec. 31, 1975.

That class action suit, brought by local Stars ticket holder Charles S. Fox, was settled in March of 1978, with Daniels agreeing to Pay a sum of $65,000 in settlement of the claims against him. The pay-out schedule was staggered, and Daniels is due to pay half the sum, $32,500, by March of 1981.

Since Daniels is planning to repay the Stars ticket holders on a dollar-for-dollar basis, beyond what the court settlement requires, Heyrend is requesting that, pending Daniels' making good on his promise, the sum already paid and currently held in trust be returned to Daniels and the $32,500 he still owes be waived. The idea, explained Heyrend, is to avoid the duplication of payment.'

Fox, the man under whose name the class action suit was filed against Daniels, was certainly a satisfied ticket holder Tuesday upon hearing the news of Daniels' plan.

"I consider his action today a truly Christian act," credited Fox.

Fox said the lawsuit was not born of bitterness or a desire to get his money back, but rather of a desire for some accountability: "The feeling was at that time that he packed his bags and left and stung the ticket holders . . . We felt if we could make an accounting, it would be a positive thing for the (sports) industry."

In terming Daniels' action an "honorable" one, Fox said, "It totally satisfies me for any of the questions I may have had."

The Salt Lake Tribune *carried an article about Bill's plan to repay ticket holders after the Utah Stars went bankrupt.*

I HAD NO LEGAL OBLIGATION TO DO WHAT I DID, BUT IT BUGGED MY CONSCIENCE. EVEN TODAY I MEET PEOPLE WHO SAY, "AREN'T YOU THE GUY WHO PAID THAT MONEY BACK TO THOSE BASKETBALL FANS IN SALT LAKE CITY ALL THOSE YEARS AGO?" IT SHOWS YOU HOW IN THE LONG TERM, HAVING ETHICS + INTEGRITY PAYS OFF.

With such high standards, it's not surprising that Bill had zero tolerance for ethical misconduct in his company. When he confirmed that two of his associates were lying about their absences from work, he fired them. He had a written code of conduct for his associates that emphasized, "Our tradition of excellence stems from one guiding value — *integrity*."

Bill had no patience for people who lacked integrity, and he made his opinions known. In 1984, he wrote to the adult son of one of his earliest business associates to scold the young man for not communicating with Bill as well as expected. Bill wrote, "I guess this letter is sort of a lecture that in the business world, 'what goes around comes around,' and if you are going to succeed you should live up to your commitments, return your phone calls, and at least have the decency to respond."

When a Denver businessman was featured in a 1992 *New York Times* article for starting yet another business that was being sued for mismanagement and fraud, Bill didn't mince words. He knew it was the latest in a series of unethical endeavors for this person. His letter said, in part:

Eventually, this is going to catch up with you. In addition to our terrible experience with you in Denver, you have been involved in two deals where the shareholders were ripped off. I honestly do not know how you can continue to live with yourself. I give a lot of time and money to the University of Denver and other places preaching the value of ethics and integrity. People like you are a great disappointment to me.

Short term, lack of integrity might be profitable to you. But long term, without ethics and integrity, it is just a matter of time until your career will end.

Someday, somehow, young man, you will get your comeuppance. My feeling is you belong behind bars. You ought to be ashamed of yourself.

Even those leading the most powerful cable and communications companies in the world were not exempt from Bill's blunt declarations of disappointment. Bill wrote to one such individual in 1994:

I am reading in the papers about the lawsuit against you. You won because the statute of limitations had expired, but the judge admonished you for not keeping your word. This makes you look bad, and somehow I would love to see this corrected. We both know that it isn't a question of whether you've got the money. It highlights a lack of integrity and ethics for not keeping your word. I feel very strongly about this. I think it is bad for your business, and it does not reflect well on our entire industry.

At times, Bill was stunned to find that others didn't share his high standards of behavior. As a voracious reader, Bill daily perused several newspapers. When he read about fraud and misconduct in companies of all sizes, it disturbed and disappointed him.

DANIELS
&ASSOCIATES INC

M E M O

Bill Daniels
CHAIRMAN

FROM: Bill Daniels

RE: University of Denver Grant

DATE: May 18, 1989

It is my desire that the University of Denver teach young men and women who wish to become leaders in business the following:

1. To be kind and considerate to all people: employees, janitors, machinists, taxi drivers, secretaries, etc., and not to act as if they are superior to any human being.

2. To understand the importance of "giving back" to society. By that I mean charity work (dollars or time), and a willingness to participate in their government at any level they choose.

3. To have good manners, both as it relates to professional courtesies and personal conduct — men to ladies and ladies to men.

4. To know the importance of punctuality.

5. To know how and when to communicate. By that I mean:
    a. Returning phone calls as soon as possible.
    b. Answering correspondence promptly.
    c. Knowing the value of thank-you notes and congratulatory notes, which are common courtesies.

6. To realize that without integrity, any career will be short-lived.

7. To know that ethics must be understood and practiced.

8. To dress and appear properly according to the profession in which they are involved.

9. To look and to be healthy and clean.

10. To be exposed to the value of small talk and other social graces that pay off during formal and informal gatherings and functions.

In conclusion, having witnessed many of our country's leading executives and political leaders, they all seem to have the above characteristics. That, along with their technical qualifications, is the primary reason those people have made it to where they are.

2930 East Third Avenue
P.O. Box 6008
Denver, Colorado 80206-0008
303 321-7550

The memo that Bill wrote outlining his expectations of what students should be taught in the Daniels College of Business at the University of Denver.

COURTESY OF BARCO LIBRARY, THE CABLE CENTER

Coincidentally, Dan Ritchie was concerned, too. (Dan was a former cable industry leader and at the time was chancellor at the University of Denver.) Discussions between the two men about this glaring void in the education system led Bill to propose funding a program at DU that would incorporate ethics and integrity into the business school curriculum. Bill was explicit about what students should be taught.

In 1994, Bill was invited to speak at the ceremony when the University of Denver announced it was renaming the business school the Daniels College of Business in his honor. He closed his remarks to the audience by saying he believed the most important legacy anyone can leave is "having family, friends, and business associates remember you as an honest person and for helping others. I believe if you live your life in this way, you'll leave this world with a clear conscience and with a smile on your face."

As it happened, one of his relatives was nearing graduation from Harvard Business School not long after Bill had read an article about the latest example of misconduct on Wall Street. Out of curiosity, Bill asked him if the school provided any instruction in ethics and integrity. At that time, the answer was *no*.

"I was appalled," Bill remembered. "I then checked with some friends of mine who had sons and daughters at Stanford, and the answer was the same: *no*. Same for Princeton, Dartmouth, Columbia, Northwestern. I could not believe it." In Bill's eyes, ethics instruction in the nation's business schools was essential to reaffirm and maintain trust in free enterprise. "Integrity in business is the ultimate competitive advantage," said Bill.

Bill believed that the combined impact of ethical lapses by people in all levels of business and the failure to educate young people on ethics and integrity was a significant threat to the American free enterprise system that he loved so much.

Putting Bill's Wishes into Practice

The Daniels Fund continues Bill's commitment to principle-based ethics instruction for students throughout their formal education. For college-level initiatives, programs must demonstrate how to apply and exemplify ethics and integrity in a business setting. This approach suggests certain guidelines for ethics instruction:

+ Understand why it matters to be ethical.

+ Develop strong, personal principles of integrity.

+ When faced with a dilemma, let those principles guide decisions.

Grounded in Bill's clear commitment to ethics, the primary objective is *active* engagement of students, not research or publishing. Specifically, the focus is on ethics instruction and real-world practical application of the high ethical principles that Bill Daniels personified.

Discussions between Bill and University of Denver Chancellor Dan Ritchie led to a program at DU that would incorporate ethics and integrity into the business school curriculum.

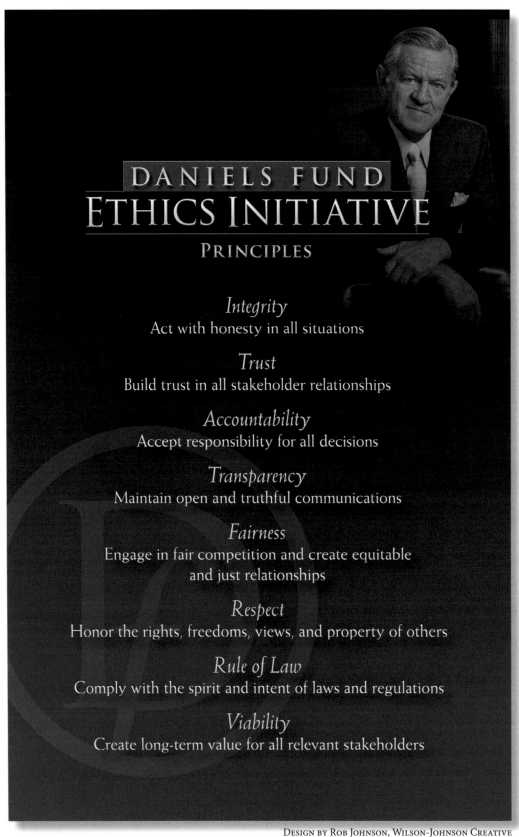

DANIELS FUND
ETHICS INITIATIVE
PRINCIPLES

Integrity
Act with honesty in all situations

Trust
Build trust in all stakeholder relationships

Accountability
Accept responsibility for all decisions

Transparency
Maintain open and truthful communications

Fairness
Engage in fair competition and create equitable
and just relationships

Respect
Honor the rights, freedoms, views, and property of others

Rule of Law
Comply with the spirit and intent of laws and regulations

Viability
Create long-term value for all relevant stakeholders

DESIGN BY ROB JOHNSON, WILSON-JOHNSON CREATIVE

The principles that guide the Daniels Fund Ethics Initiative.

The team from Colorado State University took first place in the inaugural Daniels Fund Ethics Consortium Case Competition in 2012.

CHAPTER TWENTY-ONE

HOMELESS AND DISADVANTAGED

I am for the underdog, the homeless, the hungry . . . for those who need a second chance.
~Bill Daniels

The Daniels Fund supports programs that assist homeless individuals and families in achieving and maintaining self-sufficiency through emergency services and transitional housing with supportive services.

Bill's Story

B ill Daniels sipped his freshly brewed coffee in the predawn darkness one morning in November of 1985. Safe and comfortable at home in Denver as he thumbed through the morning papers, Bill noticed an article about a homeless shelter. The feature told stories in gripping detail about the place where men addicted to drugs and alcohol got a new chance at life.

His life couldn't have been more different from the lives of those men at the shelter. With a luxurious home and a significant income, he had no worries about shelter or where his next meal would come from. In sharp contrast, the men at the shelter battled not just homelessness, but the hopelessness and lack of self-esteem that often went hand in hand with addiction.

But Bill knew something about being given a new life, and the newspaper article resonated with him at a deep level. At that time, Bill was only six months sober

One of the joys of Bill's life was helping the homeless and the hungry. Bill is pictured here with "Father Woody" of the Holy Ghost Catholic Church in Denver who dedicated his life to serving those in need.

I believe in working hard, and I have tremendous compassion for my fellow man — for those who deserve it...

I'm also totally disgusted with people who won't work. But I want to do more for those who can't.

since leaving the Betty Ford Center. He understood the power of addiction and the ongoing willpower required to overcome it. And he knew that if not for luck or the grace of God, or both, he might have followed the same path as the men at the homeless shelter.

Studying the article, Bill learned that the shelter provided temporary housing and food, along with job skills training and job placement assistance. But there were conditions. The men had to remain clean and sober, work, and pay a small fee for housing and food.

Shortly thereafter, Bill called one of his associates and instructed him to check out the shelter and find out what their needs were. Later that November, a sizable check arrived at the shelter with a note from Bill. "I want to compliment you on the fine work you are doing for men who have the desire to make it," he wrote.

Bill believed in second chances. He knew that America offers boundless opportunity, but he also understood that sometimes people need help to get started or to get back on track.

"Those of us more fortunate than others should continue to support the people who are hungry, cold, without shelter, and need a break," Bill wrote in 1987,

when he sent a contribution to a newly opened homeless shelter serving single men and women and families with children. Bill was impressed by its comprehensive services. "It is with extreme pleasure plus my thanks to God that I am able to do this," said Bill.

Growing up in the Great Depression, he experienced what it was like to lose his home. When Bill was about 10, his father's life insurance business failed, and his parents could no longer afford to rent the house where Bill had spent many of his early years. The entire family moved from Omaha, Nebraska, to Council Bluffs, Iowa, to live with Bill's grandmother. If not for the help of others, Bob and Adele Daniels and their four children might have been homeless.

However, even with a roof over their heads, the family had to be resourceful to survive. "My brother and I used to gather firewood out on the hillside to put in the furnace to keep us warm," Bill remembered. "My mother made hand lotion and sold it door-to-door, and my dad sold life insurance to farmers. Sometimes he got paid in chickens and eggs that helped feed our family."

These experiences contributed not only to Bill's drive for self-sufficiency but also to his compassion for people going through hard times. That compassion was coupled with the conviction that getting back on your feet requires not just a helping hand, but hard work. Just as his family didn't give in to despair and give up, Bill expected others in need to do their best to help themselves.

"I believe in working hard," he once said. "I have tremendous compassion for my fellow man — for those who deserve it . . . I'm also totally disgusted with people who won't work. But I want to do more for those who can't."

Never give up was a belief Bill practiced and preached. One of his secretaries at Daniels & Associates remembered that of all the gifts Bill gave his associates, the one she treasured most was a small rock painted with the words, *Pick yourself up, dust yourself off, and start over again*. Bill gave it to her in 1975, when his company was still small and going through a financial rough patch. Though an inspirational stone was all he could afford as a Christmas gift for each of his associates that year, he had no doubt that better times were ahead if everyone kept working hard and no one gave up.

Of course, Bill made it to better times, and he was generous with those less fortunate. When he learned that Monsignor C. B. "Woody" Woodrich of Holy Ghost Catholic Church was opening the church to homeless, hungry, and poor people in Denver, Bill got involved. Early one Saturday morning, he called Phil Hogue (one of his executives) and said, "Get up, get dressed, and pick me up at the office at eleven."

In the car, Bill revealed that they were going to one of Father Woody's free meals for the homeless, served in the church basement. In keeping with Bill's desire to avoid the spotlight, he handed Phil an envelope and said, "Pass this on to Woody."

Phil remembered, "We get there and the place is just full of people, and Bill proceeds to go from table to table, sitting down with these kids and moms and families with generous portions of food on their plates. We spent a couple of hours there."

On the way back, Phil asked Bill if spending time with people who had so little was uncomfortable for a man who had so much.

Without hesitation, Bill answered, "I do this as often as I can, because it reminds me of how lucky I am — and because it could just as well be me at that table."

Putting Bill's Wishes into Practice

Near the end of his life, Bill wrote to a close friend. "The joy of my life today is my good fortune in being able to help others who need help," he said. "I spend a good deal of my time on the homeless, the hungry, those who have no roof over their heads, and those who are cold because they don't have enough warm clothes."

These needs were on his mind when Bill directed the Daniels Fund to provide emergency services for individuals and families in dire circumstances.

However, Bill expected people who were given a second chance to take responsibility for their own futures, to work, and to become contributing members of society. With this goal in mind, the Daniels Fund supports programs that help people help themselves get back on their feet. Grants are available for transitional housing programs that provide a temporary place to live while providing services that help residents become self-sufficient.

RAPID RESPONSE

The Daniels Fund has a strategy for handling specific needs that fall outside of the grant areas. Though not a formal funding area, the Bill Daniels Rapid Response Fund reflects one of Bill's own giving strategies: hearing a story of someone in a personal crisis or emergency and acting on it. The Rapid Response Fund is specially designed to provide funds, which are distributed through partnerships with nonprofit agencies, for people in dire straits.

Understanding the background of Bill's commitment in this area is essential for future Daniels Fund boards.

John Saeman, an executive at Daniels & Associates, was at work in his office when Bill walked in and declared, "We need to take up a collection to help this poor guy." Bill showed John a newspaper article he'd read that morning about a man whose life depended on raising money for an organ transplant. "I've pledged $2,500," Bill added. "What can you give?"

Of course John responded with a contribution of his own, and he helped spread the word around the office. It was classic Bill Daniels. John remembered later, "He would be the first to admit that he's a very soft touch . . . Secondly, he's just loaded with empathy for his fellow man. You go and tell him a sob story, and it becomes his. He can't rest until something is done . . . I would read that article and say, 'Isn't that sad?' and move on. Bill read it and said, 'I can do something about it, and let's do it.' "

Bill's reputation for generosity resulted in numerous requests from various charities, institutions, politicians, and people in dire circumstances. But Bill had a particular soft spot for strangers. Said one of Bill's secretaries, "I think he was more touched by people he read about in the newspaper who were down on their luck than by those who approached him."

Many people tell stories of witnessing Bill's on-the-spot generosity for folks in desperate situations, and his actions were an example to the few people who knew about them. Bill's assistance to those in need even went beyond financial help. Bill once wrote, "My airplane is available to fly severely injured or ill people to specialist hospitals, and I continue to give countless gifts to worthy people." Bill kept his benevolence strictly under the radar. His preferred methods were to donate anonymously or to ask a friend to hand-deliver cash.

Dan Ritchie remembered when Bill gave away his new red Cadillac to a man who was down on his luck. "Bill was very proud of that car," Dan said. It was a symbol of success for Bill after completing one of his first big financial deals.

But when this man came to see Bill and clearly wasn't doing well, Bill said, "What you need is a change of attitude."

Dan remembered, "With that, Bill took the keys out of his pocket and said, 'Enjoy.' "

John Saeman watched Bill's generous response to an emergency even when he could not really afford it. "In 1965, we only had seven employees, and it was a constant struggle financially," said John. "But even then Bill was giving away money to people who came to him with a hard luck story. I remember one salesman from Salt Lake City who came to the office one day. I was sitting there, and he was telling a story how he needed $2,000. Well, I knew our balance sheet and how tight our finances were. But Bill wrote him out the check anyway. I asked him, 'How can you do that, just give away your money?'

"And Bill said, 'He needs it worse than I do.' "

A food bank warehouse shows the amount of space required to distribute food to communities across a state.

That same philosophy guided Bill to give big tips to wait staff, especially on holidays. Bill's niece Diane Denish told the story of watching Bill leave a $100 tip for a waitress who served them on Christmas Eve before they went home to their family. "He had a way of understanding the shoes that other people walked in," said Diane. "He understood how different that person's circumstances were from ours, and how that money could make it a little easier for her to maybe buy a toy for her daughter. He had the ability to be open-minded about other people's circumstances, to understand them."

In the rare instances when his gift wasn't accepted, Bill's offer was still remembered and appreciated. For example, June Travis, a colleague in the cable industry, got a call from Bill after her husband died. She was a young widow, and Bill was particularly concerned that she might not want to stay in her home filled with sad memories. He offered to lend her money to buy a new house. "I finally had to convince him that my existing home had more fond memories than sad ones of my husband," said June. "But it was typical of the kind of thing he would do . . . It

made me very aware that if one of my employees ran into a problem, I shouldn't be the last in line, but rather the first in line to see if there was something I could do to help."

In 1998, the people who would make up the Daniels Fund Board of Directors received the following letter from Bill:

I realize from time to time a human-interest story might be brought to your attention by another person or something you might have read in the newspaper or seen and heard in the media. In addition, you may hear of someone who needs a second chance. These situations may fit within the purpose of the Foundation. I encourage you to take a good look at them. There may be some individual or family in trouble that needs somebody's help.

The letter reminds future Daniels Fund board members of Bill's desire to take care of this unique set of needs.

Volunteers process and package donations of food to be distributed to those in need.

CHAPTER TWENTY-TWO

YOUTH DEVELOPMENT

I have supported young people all my life. I enjoy sharing my good fortune with others, but most especially young people with talent and drive.

~Bill Daniels

COURTESY OF YOUNG AMERICANS BANK

The Daniels Fund supports programs that provide opportunities for youth to develop character and gain the necessary life skills to become successful adults by funding academic and supplemental services, civic literacy and community engagement, financial literacy and entrepreneurship, and career and technical education.

Bill's Story

One of Bill Daniels' most vivid childhood memories was sitting in the living room of his family home in Omaha, Nebraska, watching his parents cry. The Great Depression had virtually

Bill supporting young entrepreneurs.

wiped out Bob Daniels' life insurance business, and he was making barely enough money to feed his wife and four children. There was no hope of paying the rent on the family home. For them — as for many others during those hard times — the outlook for the future was bleak.

Since the start of the Depression, the family had worked hard to make ends meet. But despite their best efforts, Bob and Adele were faced with the crushing realization that they needed to move to a different location where they could live more affordably.

Their best option was Council Bluffs, Iowa, where they could live with Bob's mother, a widow whose house was paid for. The move wasn't a great distance — just across the Missouri River. But for Bill, it was the leap from childhood to adulthood.

With money so tight, he felt the responsibility to help his family out as much as he could. "I was about 11 or 12 by this time," Bill remembered. "I had a newspaper route, and carried out groceries for customers at a local market. I got an idea one day that I could sell ice cream on the streets." He made his deliveries from his bicycle, keeping the ice cream cold with dry ice. "I rode all over the city of Council Bluffs," Bill said. "My best customers were mechanics in garages. I bought the ice cream in Dixie cups for a nickel and sold it for a dime."

By the time Bill was a sophomore in high school, he was working until 1:00 a.m. as a short-order cook, but still got up and went to school. He even had a job as an assistant bellboy at a hotel. "We all worked," said Bill. "We had to to survive."

Bill spoke proudly of these experiences that undoubtedly were the building blocks for the traits that came to define his business life: self-esteem

TOP | *Programs that encourage youth to explore career options are eligible for support from the Daniels Fund.* BOTTOM | *The Daniels Fund supports programs that teach youth the importance of patriotism and civic literacy.*

YOU SHOULD NEVER BE RUDE TO ANYONE. IF YOU ARE, iT WILL ALWAYS COME BACK TO HAUNT YOU.

and independence, appreciation of free enterprise, understanding the value of money, commitment to hard work and punctuality, and attention to customer service. In other words, he grew up fast, but he developed life skills and character just as quickly.

This personal development continued in military school and through Bill's years in the US Navy. "When you're in the military and you're supposed to gather at seven in the morning, that doesn't mean at 7:01; that means at 7:00, or a little earlier," remembered Bill. "Even today, I am extremely punctual, and I expect people to be punctual who are coming to see me. I learned how to concentrate, I learned neatness, I learned to keep myself clean . . . All the things I learned — not only in military school but in the Navy — have been of great use to me in my business career."

Bill recognized his ability to inspire, encourage, and mentor others. He was generous beyond words. Bill's standards were high, and he expected anyone he helped to meet his expectations.

For instance, whenever Bill contributed to a young person's education expenses, he expected a monthly report about grades, extracurricular activities, and campus involvement. And when Bill wrote to them, he didn't soften his opinions just because of their age. He could be stern but always provided guidance.

After hearing from one young man's mother about a troubling incident, Bill quickly fired off a letter to the boy:

You should never be rude to anyone, If you are, it will always come back to haunt you. You were rude to your teacher. I spend time bragging to other people about what a great kid you are. I feel like you let me down. It is not too late to correct that. I want you to write a note to your teacher apologizing for being rude, even if you apologize verbally . . . Now straighten up. You still are my best pal. I want to see good grades in addition to the above. If all of this happens, your future is unlimited. You should know that discipline is a form of love.

Jim Griesemer, then dean of the Daniels College of Business, reflected that the high expectations Bill had for young people were no different from those he had for himself. "Bill didn't expect anyone to be perfect. He wasn't perfect," said Jim. "But what he did expect was that each person would give their all to achieve whatever the goal was. And if that person was a student, your goal was to do well, to learn as much as possible, and then to

Courtesy of Young Philanthropists Foundation

Children show off the pennies they collected in a program designed to teach them the importance of helping others.

use your education, not just to make money — although that was fine — but to leave a mark on the world. Bill saw his life, I think, not simply as what he could do while he was here, but what he could leave."

Upon occasion, Bill failed to meet his own high standards, but he was quick to admit his mistake and apologize. In one letter Bill wrote to a youngster, he apologized for his thoughtlessness. "My mother taught me as a young boy to always write thank-you notes. I cannot believe I slipped up and didn't acknowledge the great little elephant that you made yourself," Bill wrote. "It sits proudly on my desk at Cableland. It is even more appreciated since I know you made it with your own two hands. Your mom reminded me yesterday that you had not heard from me, and I am terribly embarrassed. Please forgive me."

Bill's frequent messages to young people often encouraged them to be all they could be, and to keep moving forward despite seemingly insurmountable obstacles. One of his favorite stories of what a determined young person could accomplish was about a young Vietnamese immigrant named Hoang Nhu Tran who came to America in 1975 as one of the "boat people."

"He was only nine years old at the time and didn't speak a word of English," wrote Bill. "But Hoang was determined to make something out of his new life in this country. And so he has. In 1987, he graduated at the top of his class from the Air Force Academy. He then went to Oxford University as a Rhodes Scholar. He went on to attend Harvard Medical School on a full scholarship to train as a surgeon. Hoang has vowed to serve mankind and pay back many times more what America has given him. The story of Hoang Nhu Tran should be a reminder that America remains the greatest nation on earth, where boundless opportunities still exist for each and every one of us."

Bill and L.A. Express co-owner Alan Harmon spend time with young sports fans and a staffer from the team office.

Putting Bill's Wishes into Practice

Given Bill's well-documented emphasis on the importance of character-building programs for young people, the Daniels Fund carries out his wishes through a plan for youth development that focuses on Bill's values and priorities, especially programs that develop young people into productive, engaged citizens.

Throughout his life, Bill spoke widely — and wrote numerous letters — about the importance of key concepts that he felt every person should learn early and practice for a lifetime:

- ✦ Know right from wrong.
- ✦ Understand the importance of structure and discipline.
- ✦ Practice personal responsibility and accountability.
- ✦ Be a good citizen willing to give back to the community.
- ✦ Appreciate the good fortune you have to live in a free country.
- ✦ Seek an education to enable you to become a productive member of society.

With these traits as guiding principles, the Daniels Fund puts Bill's wishes into practice through Youth Development grants.

The Academic and Supplemental Services focus seeks to embody Bill's commitment to youth by preparing them for adulthood through character education and a focus on life skills. Bill knew these were essential for future success in business and in life.

The Civic Literacy and Community Engagement focus continues Bill's efforts to encourage political and community involvement. Bill stressed the need for young people to understand our democratic form of government and how communities, states, and the nation are organized. In addition, Bill wanted young people to experience how it feels to give back. Finally, Bill wished that more people would take a leadership role in their communities and in the political process.

The Financial Literacy and Entrepreneurship focus maintains the commitment Bill Daniels had to financial education and programs to promote free enterprise. He wanted to give young people a broader understanding of how their own experiences with finance fit into the bigger picture.

The Career and Technical Education focus supports career development, mentoring, and employment programs that put young people on the path to independence through work.

Bill with the granddaughter of a friend.

PART FIVE

YOUNG AMERICANS BANK

CHAPTER TWENTY-THREE

HANDS-ON LESSONS IN FREE ENTERPRISE

*I have always felt the best way to teach kids about money management
is to let them do it — with real money.*

~ Bill Daniels

COURTESY OF YOUNG AMERICANS BANK

Bill Daniels defined a unique arrangement for ongoing support from his foundation, the Daniels Fund, to Young Americans Bank, his bank designed to prepare kids to prosper in our free enterprise system.

Banks can be intimidating. That's what Bill Daniels experienced the first time he walked into a bank at age 24. "I felt like I was going in for brain surgery or as a defendant in a murder trial," he remembered. "I was *that* intimidated."

Bill was reminded of that experience when, in 1984, he read a newspaper article about a fifth-grade class wanting to do a project that would cost roughly $200. Rather than do a fundraiser, their teacher thought it would be a better learning experience if they went to a bank to see if they could borrow the money.

Bill proudly stands with the group of teenagers who were hired to spread the word about the bank opening and encourage merchants to put decals in their windows saying, "Young Americans Bank Checks Welcome Here."

As Bill told the story, "The bank threw them out. My God, what could they have been thinking? It doesn't take a rocket scientist to see our young people aren't being armed with the tools they need to be truly successful in our free enterprise system, at least not without making a lot of mistakes along the way, like I did. Hell, these kids are going to be running *my* company someday. And I want it done right." Bill decided the best way to teach these financial skills was to open a bank for kids.

The extraordinary result of Bill's vision is Young Americans Bank.

It is important that future Daniels Fund board members understand how Young Americans Bank was created, its unique banking regulatory status, and why Bill directed the Daniels Fund to carry on his personal commitment to the bank.

Although Bill never expected the bank to be profitable, he always intended it to be a real, regulated, commercial bank. This required years of planning and creative problem solving. His determination never wavered. In order to achieve his vision, Bill made unprecedented commitments to state and federal regulators who ultimately agreed to take a chance on this unique banking concept on the strength of Bill's promise to cover its losses, if necessary.

Why a Bank for Kids?

Bill was clear about his intentions. "I want our bank to show kids how to conduct everyday banking transactions," he said, "to save money, to borrow money, to learn about investment options, and to establish a credit history so they're better prepared to participate in the free enterprise system and understand the workings of business." Bill believed America's financial system was the best in the world. He wanted young people to understand it in order to benefit from it.

Bill also wanted them to have a positive banking

> bill daniels
>
> IT DOESN'T TAKE A ROCKET SCIENTIST TO SEE OUR YOUNG PEOPLE AREN'T BEING ARMED WITH THE TOOLS THEY NEED TO BE TRULY SUCCESSFUL IN OUR FREE ENTERPRISE SYSTEM, AT LEAST NOT WITHOUT MAKING A LOT OF MISTAKES ALONG THE WAY, LIKE I DID.
>
> HELL, THESE KIDS ARE GOING TO BE RUNNING MY COMPANY SOMEDAY. AND I WANT IT DONE RIGHT!

experience at a young age, so that they would know how to use banking relationships in their adult lives and future careers. Armed with knowledge, these young people would grow up to be better employees and entrepreneurs, taxpayers and citizens.

Bill felt that only through real-life banking experiences could the kids learn those lessons. His vision was more far-reaching than a credit union or offering banking classes. He wanted nothing less than a real commercial bank, offering actual banking products.

From the beginning, Bill's intention was for the bank to serve only young people, not their parents or teachers. At times, people suggested adding adult customers to make the bank more self-sustaining. But Bill believed if adult customers were intermixed with young customers, the focus would drift from educating kids and toward processing quick transactions. He insisted on a state-chartered, FDIC-insured, commercial bank for kids.

A bank was, by far, the most difficult route he could have chosen.

Overcoming Regulatory Hurdles

Bill wanted a state charter so that he could know the Colorado regulators and work closely with them. That state charter required FDIC insurance, and that brought in another group of regulators. This meant that lots of people who knew banking much better than Bill were now taking a critical look at his idea and shaking their heads. The regulators just could not wrap their heads around the concept of a bank for kids.

At first, regulators didn't take Bill seriously. They were, of course, skeptical of a bank for kids who would presumably maintain only very small balances in their accounts. The regulators did not believe such a bank would ever be able to sustain itself.

Bill was undeterred. He was prepared and willing to meet their concerns head on. Knowing that regulators required a bank's executive management team to include people with proven banking experience, one of Bill's first actions was to hire top-notch people to help him. Among the first people recruited was Linda Childears, an independent consultant who brought a strong résumé in banking and finance.

The banking climate in the mid-1980s was tough. The failure of nearly 750 savings and loan associations — at a cost to the taxpayers of roughly $125 billion — resulted in tighter oversight by regulators.

As Young Americans Bank was being developed, regulators were closing 10 banks a week across the nation. During this time period, 70 banks were closed in Colorado alone.

It was not an environment conducive to new, and potentially risky, concepts in banking. In the best of times, regulators would have been wary of Bill's idea. Given the fact that they were drowning in paperwork for bank closings, it was an especially bad time for them to consider this highly unusual request.

Since their job is to protect consumers and the banking system, the regulators require banks to maintain levels of capital to cover any operating losses. Banks must be profitable to build and maintain working capital. But Bill did not expect Young Americans Bank to be profitable. The dilemma was how to resolve two such contradictory objectives.

Bill responded that he would personally back the bank with his own money and fund projected losses before they occurred. This impressed the regulators, but they feared Bill would lose passion for the project at some point and stop funding it. To them, it was almost beyond belief that Bill was more motivated to educate children about banking than to earn a profit. They pointed to other concerns as well. All banking transactions are legal contracts, but these customers would mostly be minors. If the regulators approved this unprecedented idea and it failed, not only would they look foolish but

Bill poses next to State Banking Commissioner Richard Doby as they hold the bank's official charter.

also the customers involved in the bank failure would all be children. The repercussions of such a scenario were painful to contemplate.

Bill understood that he was asking bank regulators to stick their necks out for this concept, and he assured them that his bank would comply 110 percent. "And we did," Linda remembered. "Most banks don't want to talk to their regulators. We made a point of it. We had them in all the time and really kept them involved in what we were doing. They knew who we were and that we truly respected their perspectives."

In addition to his pledge to personally maintain necessary capital levels, Bill further promised that his commitment to the bank would be written into his estate-planning documents. As the bank's sole shareholder, he would review the operations every year. If the bank were to become no longer viable — such as if a law were passed to prohibit minors from having bank accounts — Bill committed to assist the federal government in an orderly shutdown that would not incur a loss to the FDIC.

It would take two and a half years and two application denials before regulators were convinced. They granted approval for Young Americans Bank in July of 1987.

Making the Vision a Reality

Shortly before the approval, Linda's role changed from consultant to bank president. When she found out that Bill wanted to open just a few months later — on Colorado Day, the first Monday in August — she was apprehensive, but inspired. Making all the adjustments that were necessary to ready the bank for kids was a monumental task, but everyone was up for the challenge. They had to be.

All the "traditional" banking forms had to be customized and simplified for younger people. Smaller bodies dictated that adjustments needed to be made to the physical space. For instance, to accommodate young customers, counters were lowered, kid-friendly

Counters at Young Americans Bank could accommodate youth of all heights.

seating areas were designed, and plenty of candy was placed at each teller window. Everything needed to be designed with the customer in mind.

"But no matter what obstacle we encountered," Linda remembered, "we'd hear the same thing from Bill, 'So what's your point? Fix it.' I became personally caught up in how exciting it was to conquer these little issues one at a time and make this thing happen."

Another top priority was to hire skilled, knowledgeable people who also loved working with kids. Each new hire went through intensive training about how business would be conducted in this one-of-a-kind bank.

Business etiquette was always very important to Bill, and he wanted the same high standards at the bank as he had in his other businesses. He insisted that bank personnel would greet all customers warmly and shake their hands. Every transaction was to be treated as a learning experience, and the focus was to always be on the kids, and not on the parents or other adults who brought them into the bank.

Another pressing issue was to persuade merchants to accept checks from Young Americans Bank customers. Bill expressed this concern early: "What would happen if these 12-year-olds walked out of our lobby with a checkbook and went into a store — feeling empowered and excited about their checking account — and no retailer would accept their checks?"

Anticipating that reaction, the bank hired a dozen teenagers to visit local stores and shopping centers to educate merchants about the new bank and encourage them to put a decal in the window saying "Young Americans Bank Checks Welcome Here." Before long, retailers were calling the bank to ask, "How do I get one of those stickers?"

Bill wanted the young customers to have access to simple but up-to-date products. Some of the initial offerings were savings and checking accounts as well as certificates of deposit. Recognizing that most of the young customers wouldn't have driver's licenses, the bank also issued photo ID cards right in the lobby.

Later, credit cards (with a $100 credit limit) were added to the product mix. The goals were to deglamorize credit, teach young people what powerful financial tools credit cards are, and to teach them how to manage their credit well. The customers at Young Americans Bank handled their credit cards wonderfully, but there was significant pushback from the media for offering credit cards to minors.

Concerned that Americans were not saving money at the rate that people in other nations were, Bill made building a positive savings habit one of his objectives. Another important goal was for people from different cultural and economic backgrounds to have access to this banking experience. The staff worked hard at reaching all economic levels, including kids whose parents didn't use banks.

Young Americans Bank welcomed its first customers on August 3, 1987. The worldwide media attention for the

A new customer opens an account at Young Americans Bank.

grand opening was astounding. Marketing was important to Bill, and he invested $250,000 of his own money — not bank funds — for pre-opening publicity to bring customers into the bank.

He wanted people all over the world to know about the bank, and he got his wish. The bank opening was major news in *USA Today*, the *Washington Post*, and newspapers as far away as Hong Kong and West Germany. It was also featured in *Newsweek* and other magazines. Television and radio stations carried stories about the bank, too.

The three-week grand opening celebration was exciting and fun, but there were a few glitches. One problem was that the bank's first three coin-counting machines couldn't keep up with all the kids bringing in their piggy banks.

Nearly 2,000 accounts were opened during the grand opening period. By the end of the third month, 5,000 accounts had been established.

Bill's personal — as well as financial — interest in the bank was substantial. One morning in August of 1988, two young boys were opening accounts as Bill stood in the lobby, observing them in the midst of the typical hustle and bustle of the busy bank. Noticing the two boys with their piggy banks and a shoebox full of change, he walked over to them. "Hi there. I'm Bill Daniels, the owner of this bank," he told them. "Tomorrow will be the first anniversary of our grand opening. In celebration of the anniversary, here's some money to help those accounts." He presented each of them with a $100 bill.

Personal and business loans were offered, and many budding entrepreneurs took advantage of them. Early customers took out loans to purchase puppies, personal computers, and used cars. They also borrowed money to fund business ventures, but only after they submitted a written business plan. The new entrepreneurs financed ventures such as a recording studio, a herd of dairy goats, and a hand-painted sweatshirt enterprise.

One young business owner was even interviewed on the *Today* show. When the host asked what he'd learned

TOP | *A young customer with her savings register.* CENTER | *Young Americans Bank welcomed its first customers on August 3, 1987 to worldwide media attention.* BOTTOM | *The ribbon-cutting ceremony at the opening of Young Americans Bank.*

from his experience and if there were any surprises, he responded, "Well, yeah. Did you know they want more money back than what you borrowed?"

In time, debit cards, ATM services, and access to online banking were offered, too. And the services keep expanding.

Extending the Educational Mission

For Bill Daniels, the success of Young Americans Bank was not measured by the bottom line, but by how many young customers the bank had and the richness of their experience. By its fifth anniversary, the bank had 15,640 accounts. More than 90 percent of them were savings accounts. By the end of 2011, nearly 70,000 accounts had been opened.

Although Bill was never interested in franchising the bank, he hoped that others would want to replicate the idea in their own communities. Young Americans Bank soon had young customers from all 50 states and more than a dozen foreign countries.

As more people learned about Young Americans Bank, educators sought help in developing supplemental

Linda Childears and Bill celebrate the first anniversary of Young Americans Bank with one of the bank's customers.

programs to teach free enterprise and financial skills to their students. The bank responded and worked with educators to develop relevant programs.

The popularity and success of these educational programs led to the creation in 1989 of a companion 501(c)(3) nonprofit, Young Americans Education Foundation (YAEF). It assumed the delivery of financial literacy programs that expanded and complemented the educational lessons learned at the bank. While Bill was personally committed to funding the bank — and he seeded the new nonprofit — YAEF's continuing operations were funded by the community through donations, grants, and program fees.

YAEF partnered with educators to develop a classroom curriculum for children in fifth and sixth grades. It taught concepts such as supply and demand, job skills and work habits, banking procedures, democratic processes, civic consciousness, and career awareness. The curriculum culminates in a day at Young AmeriTowne — a model town where students operate numerous businesses to practice for future roles like electing officials, paying bills, and marketing products.

Bank customers who were two years old were presented with cakes in 1989 at the second anniversary of YAB's opening.

Specially designed facilities in Denver and Lakewood, Colorado, were added to expand the Young AmeriTowne experience. An affiliated Rural AmeriTowne program was opened in Wray, Colorado, to serve students in eastern Colorado, Kansas, and Nebraska.

Financial literacy programs for youth of all ages have expanded to cover personal finance, free enterprise, entrepreneurship, and global economics. Some are taught in schools while other topics are offered at other sites and summer camps. In its first 25 years, the bank and its companion programs have served nearly half a million children.

Planning for the Future

In the early years of Young Americans Bank, Bill Daniels was the sole shareholder of the bank and personally subsidized its budgeted loss each year. When he began his estate-planning process, he faced significant challenges in creating a sustaining structure for Young Americans Bank. However, as usual, these challenges were overcome by unprecedented solutions.

First, Bill needed to transfer ownership of the bank to an entity, since he obviously could not be the sole shareholder after his death. When an entity, rather than an individual, owns a bank, that entity becomes a bank holding company. Bank holding companies are subject to another significant layer of regulations.

It was determined that a private foundation like the one Bill was planning for his estate would have a difficult time meeting the regulations required of a bank holding company. In short, it would have meant that the Daniels Fund would always have to be run by qualified bankers. And the Daniels Fund's charitable mission focus is not compatible with what would have been acceptable to banking regulations.

To avoid those problems, Bill decided in 1990 to donate his bank stock to the Young Americans Education Foundation. He personally guaranteed to continue funding the bank's losses as long as he was alive. Bill stipulated that after he died, his charitable foundation would fund YAEF annually with a grant. This money would then be used by YAEF to inject capital into Young Americans Bank ahead of projected losses.

Such a strategy had never been tried before. But could it get approved? This brought a third regulatory entity into the picture, the Federal Reserve System, with the responsibility of overseeing bank holding companies. When they reviewed the idea, they pointed out that

---

A panoramic view of Young AmeriTowne, a model town where students operate numerous businesses to practice for future roles like electing officials, paying bills, and marketing products.

TOP | *The original location of Young Americans Bank was at 250 Steele Street in Denver.* CENTER | *The second location was at 311 Steele Street.* BOTTOM | *The bank is now located at 3550 East 1st Avenue.*

holding companies usually must provide added financial strength to the banks they own. YAEF was a nonprofit with no real financial strength. But with the Daniels Fund guaranteeing donations to YAEF to ensure capitalization of the bank, the Federal Reserve Board was persuaded to approve the arrangement. Once again, regulators took a chance, enabling Young Americans Bank to continue its mission on behalf of kids.

It became clear that YAEF needed to separate the financial statements of its nonprofit education programs from the bank's financial reporting.

Showing ownership of a bank in YAEF's financial statements made it difficult to raise funds for the financial literacy programs. In response, a new 501(c)(3), the Young Americans Center for Financial Education (YACFE), was formed in 2001 to house educational programs. YAEF remained the bank holding company and became the umbrella organization for both the bank and YACFE, each of which has its own separate auditors.

At the moment of Bill's death in March of 2000, the FDIC was literally in the building conducting an examination of the bank. They were understandably concerned about how Bill's death might impact the bank's future. Fortunately, Bill had anticipated this, and his foundation's board knew his expectations. The board met right away and assured regulators that the Daniels Fund would continue to provide the same support that Bill had provided in his lifetime.

Additionally, in his will Bill left a $6 million endowment to Young Americans Education Foundation

to help support the bank. He knew the endowment would give comfort to regulators, but he also knew the ongoing support from the Daniels Fund was crucial. Bill was unsure how large an endowment might be needed to support the bank, and he wanted the Daniels Fund to serve in an oversight role.

The Daniels Fund adopted a policy that requires an annual review of Young Americans Bank against the guiding principles that were so important to Bill. If the bank were to stray from those principles or cease to be viable, the Daniels Fund could opt to discontinue its support. In that case, the Daniels Fund would notify regulators as required in its commitment letter.

The Daniels Fund board understands Bill's intent for the bank. It also recognizes the regulatory approvals required to establish Young Americans Bank were extremely difficult to achieve and that regulator confidence must be maintained.

When Bill was inducted into the Colorado Business Hall of Fame in 1996, he was asked what accomplishment in his life he was most proud of. He replied, "Young Americans Bank."

Bill Daniels supported many causes in the community, but there were only two charitable ventures that he personally initiated: Young Americans Bank and the Daniels Fund. He intended both to last forever.

DANIELS FUND

August 23, 2000

Board of Directors, Young Americans Bank
Board of Directors, Young Americans Education Foundation
Colorado Division of Banking
Federal Deposit Insurance Corporation
Federal Reserve Bank of Kansas City

Ladies and Gentlemen:

Bill Daniels, the founder and benefactor of Young Americans Bank (YAB), passed away on March 7, 2000. This letter sets forth the intention of the Daniels Fund to support YAB in light of this development.

As you know, during Mr. Daniels' lifetime, he made annual contributions to Young Americans Education Foundation (YAEF), the parent company of YAB, equal to the bank's projected operating deficit for the upcoming year. In his estate planning, Mr. Daniels established two mechanisms that will serve to support YAB. First, he made a $6 million endowment bequest ("Endowment") to YAEF, the income from which is to directly support YAB. Second, he expressly identified YAB (via assistance to YAEF) as a specific activity to be funded by his personal foundation, the Daniels Fund, as long as the bank's activities are viewed by the IRS as having a qualified charitable purpose.

Mr. Daniels' estate is in the process of being settled. The bulk of Mr. Daniels' assets will be transferred to the Daniels Fund. At current market values, the Daniels Fund is expected to have in excess of $1 billion in assets, with an annual distribution requirement of at least $50 million.

This letter is to set forth the plan of the Daniels Fund and our intention to assume Mr. Daniels' role in providing ongoing support for YAB. Our goal is to assist YAB in: a) covering any annual deficit in its operations; and, b) maintaining a "well-capitalized" status under current banking law, including a tier 1 leverage ratio of 6%.

Prior to the beginning of each calendar year, we will evaluate YAB's and YAEF's achievements to-date and any projected operating deficit for the upcoming year. We reserve the right to evaluate YAB's and YAEF's financial performance and fulfillment of their mission of educating young people.

55 Madison Street, Suite 255 · Denver, CO 80206 · tel 303.393.7220 · fax 303.393.7339 · toll free 877.791.4726

In the absence of a notice to you, we agree to provide YAEF an amount equal to YAB's projected operating deficit (including bank related expenses incurred by YAEF), less the projected income on the Endowment and projected contributions from other sources, for the upcoming year ("Losses"). We agree to fund these Losses periodically throughout the year, in advance of their incurrence. If actual Losses are less than projected Losses, the difference will be netted against future contributions. If actual Losses exceed projected Losses, we will make an additional contribution in the current year. We will notify you in writing prior to the beginning of that year if our decision is not to fund (a decision which we do not presently contemplate).

With respect to maintaining a "well-capitalized" status under current banking law, including a tier 1 leverage ratio of 6%, we agree either: a) to provide YAEF an amount required to maintain such status and leverage ratio for YAB; or, b) to assist YAEF in voluntarily liquidating YAB, if YAEF determines that funding is insufficient to continue YAB's operations. Until an orderly dissolution is complete, we will assist YAEF and YAB in maintaining required capital levels. In any liquidation plan, after utilization by YAB of its capital and after utilization by YAEF of all remaining funds in the Endowment, we will pay all remaining balances owed to YAB's depositors that are not covered by FDIC.

This pledge is consistent with Mr. Daniels' financial support of YAB in the past. This commitment may be relied upon by YAB and YAEF, and by the regulators and Board of Directors of each organization.

Sincerely,

Daniels Fund Board of Directors

John W. (Jack) Daniels, Chairman   Phillip J. Hogue, President

---

A letter written shortly after Bill's death in 2000 outlines the commitment of the Daniels Fund to support Young Americans Bank.

PART SIX

THE WISDOM
OF BILL DANIELS

CHAPTER TWENTY-FOUR

IN BILL'S OWN WORDS

I have a confession for you, God. You have provided me with a hell of a life.
Some good and some bad, but I've had a ball.

~ Bill Daniels

Throughout his life, Bill offered words of encouragement and advice through his letters, speeches, and conversations. It was important to him to share his knowledge and values, not just with his own generation, but with the next generations as well. Here are a few of the nuggets of wisdom that defined Bill Daniels.

Bill, in a photo taken in the late 1970s.

Live a life of meaning.

When you put your life in perspective, you realize how little time there is to make something truly significant out of it. To some people, this might mean acquiring a lot of possessions. To others, building a business or owning property. And there are those whose lives won't be fulfilled unless they achieve fame and fortune. There's nothing wrong with any of these aspirations. But, for me, they pale in comparison to individuals who want to leave something more consequential as their legacy.

Give.

Imagine a world where people give of themselves simply because they want to. Not out of a sense of debt. Or because they want something in return. No ulterior motives. No feelings of guilt. Just the desire to give for the sake of giving. Now, instead of imagining this kind of world, do your part in making it happen. Make a charitable donation. Volunteer your time to improve your community. Give back to the world that gives so much to you. And if it happens to make you feel good to give, that's all right. Feeling good is the one ulterior motive that's acceptable.

Count your blessings and share them.

Each person on this planet is unique. Each with a spirit of their own. Each with blessings to count. Share your special love with your family and friends. Take a quiet half-hour by yourself from time to time to count all the things you have to be thankful for.

Take care of those less fortunate.

Why not share your good fortune with those around you? Take an hour out of your schedule and pay a visit to an elderly neighbor. Find a way to help a family that is homeless. Put a couple extra coins in the Salvation Army's kettle during the holidays. There are no luggage racks on hearses. You can't take it with you.

Treat all people with dignity.

The lowest-ranked person should be treated with the same dignity and respect as the first vice president. I think something happens to people who got lucky and succeeded. All of a sudden they have a big ego and think they are geniuses and lose touch with the common man. I have never forgotten where I came from. I treat everybody the same whether they are the janitor, bellman, waitress, mail clerk, or whoever. Remember: God created all of us as equals.

Have class.

One quality I admire most in a person is class. I'm not referring to the title on their business card or their financial rating. It has nothing to do with the style of their clothes or the car they drive. To me, class is something you choose for yourself. It's competing honestly, confronting problems head-on, taking accolades with grace and humility, and not knocking your competitors. If you have class, you are loyal to both yourself and to those around you. Class is born out of self-respect and a healthy respect for others. Everything in this world is not always attainable. Fortunately, class is. Wouldn't it be a better world if, one day, we all decided to have it?

Believe in yourself.

It has made millionaires out of paupers. It has earned the Nobel Prize. And by using it wisely, entrepreneurs have ended up running corporations. I'm referring to believing in yourself and your ideas. Taking a chance on your own merit and giving the world your best shot. Somebody once said, "Observe the turtle. He progresses only with his neck out." I think the same holds true for us two-legged creatures. If you've never taken a chance on yourself, at least think about it. Unless you do, you may never know what you're missing out on. And neither will the rest of the world.

You never know.

You never know who's going to sit next to you on an airplane. You never know who you might meet at a cocktail party or on a train. Learn how to talk to people, then listen to what they have to say. Get to know a little bit about them and what makes them tick. Find common ground and interesting things to talk about. If you don't make an effort to reach out and discover good qualities in people, someone who could have been a great friend or business relationship will be gone and out of your life before they ever got a chance to enter it. I've made some great friends this way, and even had casual conversations that turned into million-dollar business deals. You never know.

Bill in his office in 1983.

Don't make assumptions based on a person's appearance.

How many times have you passed judgment on someone based strictly on first appearances? Many years ago, I walked into a Cadillac dealership in Denver on a Saturday afternoon. I was unshaven and wearing a baseball cap, shorts, and sandals. I asked the salesman on the floor if he could tell me the price of the car I was looking at. His reply was, "You couldn't afford it." Over the next 40 years, I have probably bought two dozen Cadillacs, but I have never gone back to the place where the salesman uttered those words. What makes people special isn't their physical appearance or the clothes they wear. It's their personal values, ideas, and the way they choose to conduct their lives.

Always tell the truth.

I just tell people the truth. If I tell the truth, I never have to remember what I told anyone.

Learn table manners.

I thought I knew table manners; my mother used to work me over pretty good. And then I had to go to New York, and I'd go to these fancy dinners and fancy restaurants, and I'd see four forks over here, three knives over here, a knife up here, four different glasses, a napkin folded different than I'd ever seen it, and I had to observe people to find out what to do. I was having dinner with these bankers and potential partners who I wanted to impress, so I had to pay attention. Be smart and learn table manners before you get put in an embarrassing situation.

Write thank-you notes.

Always acknowledge people's kindness to you with a written note, preferably on paper, in an envelope, sent through the mail. Your thoughtfulness will go a long way.

Dress properly for the occasion.

Dress properly within your budget. Make sure your clothes are clean and well pressed. Have your shoes shined. Comb your hair. It doesn't sound very important, but I can tell you it is.

Bill, at his desk in the Daniels Communications Center.

Have integrity.

You didn't tell on your brother when you were a kid. Loyalty was more important to you than scoring points with your parents. If you got a bad grade, you stood in front of your father with your report card and took your punishment. Instead of asking for spending money, you chose to earn it. In college, you stood up for what you believed in. You didn't lie to get the job. And you never compromised your ideals to keep it. You're the kind of person who might take the blame to help out a friend, but you'd never take credit for an accomplishment that wasn't yours. Integrity isn't something you get overnight. It takes a lifetime to earn.

Be disciplined.

If you didn't mow the lawn, you didn't get your allowance. You told a lie and got grounded for a week. If you weren't a team player, you sat on the bench. It's called discipline. And it's not only an important part of growing up, it's an important part of your entire life. Discipline teaches us to respect authority as well as command it. And it gives us the mettle to make tough decisions in just about every situation. Discipline is why military personnel and athletes go on to become so successful in business. Nobody likes to be disciplined. But it's something you learn to appreciate when you realize the positive effect it has on your life.

Be courteous with everyone at work.

All too often people in high places forget where they came from. And while they make every effort to treat their peers and superiors with friendliness and respect, they don't always afford others the same common courtesy. Next time you have an opportunity, why not ask a new employee what his or her aspirations are for the future. Or give a few words of encouragement to your secretary or someone on your staff. You have the ability to make people happy with just a few thoughtful words. Why not start using them?

Appreciate and care for your employees.

I've always told people that they don't work for me, they work with me. And that means things like respect and courtesy go both ways. People want more than a paycheck for their efforts. They want to know you care about them. They want you to listen to their ideas, to be open to their suggestions, and to provide them with a good office environment. Most of all, they want you to offer criticism when necessary and a pat on the back when they deserve it. There's a common misconception in the workplace. People always feel they have to please the boss. If a company is to be truly successful, it has to be the other way around. Treat people right, not just because they'll be better employees, but because it's the right thing to do.

Plow profits back into your community and company.

The money companies earn is called profit. It's used for a variety of things. But the finest companies plow profits back into the community. They give contributions to needy organizations and individuals. They sponsor charitable events. They refurbish their offices and grounds. And something miraculous happens! The money they "gave away" comes back tenfold in long-term profits, because their customers gained a greater appreciation and loyalty for their products and services. And who's going to argue with 10-to-one odds?

Don't be afraid to fail.

Never criticize someone for trying something new and failing. It comes with the territory. To get ahead in business and in life, you better be willing to push the envelope a little bit. Where there are opportunities, there are often challenges. Don't be put off by the sheer size of them. Very few successful people haven't had to face difficult challenges along the way. But a business reversal or personal setback will often bring out the best in a person and enable them to find courage and strength they never even knew they possessed. In these uncertain times, there's always a chance you might find yourself in a similar situation. Nevertheless, if you genuinely believe in yourself, I'll bet you have what it takes to turn things around for the better.

Neither a scrooge nor a patsy be.

Why is it that when people enter into business negotiations they feel they have to act in a certain way? A plaque in my office reads, "Neither a scrooge nor a patsy be." This motto has taught me a lot of lessons. You have to be solid and upstanding in your principles and ideals. Strong in the board room. Shrewd in negotiations. But also make it a point to be compassionate and understanding. Listen to what the other person has to say. And give more than you have to. If you're really going to find success in this world, you need to remember there's a time to be tough and a time to be tender.

OPPOSITE | *A mid 1980s photo of Bill.* Photo by Nicholas DeSciose

Admit when you don't know.

All too often, some people are afraid to admit they don't have all the answers. So they just make them up. They elaborate on what they don't understand to the point of embarrassment. Instead, all they had to do was say, "I don't know, but I'll find out." Remember, nobody can fault you for admitting you don't know everything. In fact, they might even admire you.

Understand the secrets of success.

I was often asked what I thought were the secrets to success. Here they are in a nutshell:

1. Contacts, contacts, contacts. Know everyone and something about them, including the names of their family members.

2. Be visible and get involved in your trade association and leadership organizations.

3. Always maintain integrity.

4. Perform, perform, perform.

If you do those four things, you will have the world by the ass.

Be neat and clean.

Perhaps it was my training in military school and the Navy, but I insist that everything stay in its place and that buildings be spotlessly clean. You will show the proper respect for others by keeping your own work areas neat, clean, and tidy at all times.

Give a good handshake.

Please, please learn to give a good handshake when you shake hands. If I'm interviewing you for a job, whether you're a man or woman, and I meet you for the first time, I don't like to put my hand around a wet fish. I don't think anybody does.

Be on time.

Learn to be punctual. I don't care where you're working, if you're not punctual, you're gone. I make it a point to arrive at my appointments two to three minutes early.

Return all correspondence and telephone calls promptly.

I return all of my phone calls. Some calls I don't want to make, because I know what the call is about, but I do it.

Be loyal.

Be loyal to your boss and your colleagues in your company and associations.

Step away from electronics and interact personally with people.

New technology is making our lives better in many ways. At work, computers process information in milliseconds, and we communicate around the globe with the touch of a few buttons. At home, we have dozens of entertainment and communications options. And even more impressive services will soon be added to our televisions and telephones. But while technology has the ability to put us in touch with each other at lightning speed, it also has the potential to separate us if we're not careful. You just might want to step away from all the electronic gadgets and get some fresh air. Visit your co-workers down the hall, or your neighbors down the street. Better yet, volunteer your time to help someone in your community less fortunate than yourself. Technology can do a lot of things for us, but not nearly as much as we can do for each other.

Acknowledge people.

One of the worst insults in life is not to acknowledge the presence of another. Making someone feel that they're not significant can hurt someone beyond measure. Greet people warmly when you see them, and make them feel special. They are.

Live your life so that you can leave it with a clear conscience and a smile on your face.

Be the kind of person who takes the time to pass on knowledge and values to the next generation. Strive to live your life such that family, friends, and business associates remember you as an honest person. Help others who will be left behind. I believe if you live your life in this way, you'll leave this world with a clear conscience and with a smile on your face.

EPILOGUE

Every person who has worked diligently on this story hopes that you have enjoyed reading it as much as we have enjoyed telling it. By reading the stories and lessons of this great man, perhaps you will understand Bill Daniels better and the reasons why he worked so hard to create a foundation that would carry his wishes into the future, to the benefit of thousands and thousands of people.

This book is written for future board members and associates in an effort to convey the importance of adhering to the intent of a man who put so much thought, word, and deed into establishing the Daniels Fund and to honor the legacy of the man who initiated it.

OPPOSITE | *Bill beams in this 1985 photograph.*   PHOTO BY NICHOLAS DeSCIOSE

On February 28, 1995. Bill's Learjet 35-A became the first private aircraft to land at Denver International Airport. Bill was aboard the aircraft, piloted by Mark Calkins, when it landed shortly after midnight. The jet, named Cablevision Tool, was donated to the City of Denver and is suspended in Concourse C at DIA.

REFERENCES

Chapter One

Opening quote — "I've lived a fantastic life . . .": Letter from Bill to Gene Clark, January 21, 1981.

Chapter Two

Opening quote — "My mother used to tell people what a gentleman . . .": Letter from Bill to Lorraine Scholtz, Parsippany, New Jersey, December 13, 1993.

"My dad was a super salesman": Letter from Bill to Bob Delbridge, October 30, 1993.

Peanut machines and selling magazines: "Bill Daniels: The Father of Cable TV" oral history interview by Max Paglin, conducted February 10, 1986, for The Cable Center's Hauser Oral and Video History Collection.

Genealogical information on Bill's parents: Singular, Stephen. (2003). *Relentless: Bill Daniels and the Triumph of Cable TV*. The Bill Daniels Estate, p. 20.

Examples of tough times during Depression: "Bill Daniels: The Father of Cable TV" oral history interview by Max Paglin, conducted February 10, 1986, for The Cable Center's Hauser Oral and Video History Collection; Letter from Bill to Bob Delbridge, October 30, 1993.

Bill's jobs: "Bill Daniels: The Father of Cable TV" oral history interview by Max Paglin, conducted February 10, 1986, for The Cable Center's Hauser Oral and Video History Collection; Mohler, J. C. "A Biography: This Is Bill Daniels." Publication unknown, circa 1974.

Bill was an altar boy: Letter from Bill to Wayne Harding, Denver, September 17, 1987.

Dick Caughlan going to confession: Letter from Bill to Zeph Telpner, Council Bluffs, December 9, 1993.

Jack Daniels recounts Bill's street-fighting behavior: Singular, Stephen. "Wired for Success: Denver's Cable King Bill Daniels Knows What Makes Television Work — Money." *Empire Magazine* of the *Denver Post, March 20, 1983.*

Adele Daniels' schooling: Letter from Bill to Margolyn Woods, November 22, 1999.

Manners Bill learned from his mother: Letter from Bill to Letitia Baldrige, May 7, 1997.

Family move to Hobbs: Letter from Bill to Howard G. Klein, San Antonio, April 29, 1993; New Mexico Community Foundation profile of Jack Daniels and family, circa 2003.

Adele's first impression of Hobbs: New Mexico Community Foundation profile of Jack Daniels and family, circa 2003.

The Daniels children didn't like Hobbs at first: New Mexico Community Foundation profile of Jack Daniels and family, circa 2003.

Bill liked to watch his parents sing and dance: Letter from Bill to Bob Delbridge, July 1, 1998.

Hobbs was a rough-and-tumble town: Smith, Brad. "Bill Daniels: The Life and Times of the King of Cable." *Colorado Business*, August 1994.

"I was kind of a wild ass": Letter from Bill to Howard G. Klein, April 29, 1998.

Chapter Three

Opening quote — "I thought I was the toughest . . .": Smith, Brad. "Bill Daniels: The Life and Times of the King of Cable." *Colorado Business*, August 1994.

"I am far from perfect": Letter from Bill to Cadet Cameron Gray, New Mexico Military Institute, August 17, 1989.

Virtues Bill learned at NMMI: Letter from Bill to Major Alfred L. Castle, NMMI, August 26, 1983; Letter from Bill to Cadet Cameron Gray, New Mexico Military Institute, August 17, 1989.

Nickname "Jeep": Singular, Stephen. (2003). *Relentless: Bill Daniels and the Triumph of Cable TV*. The Bill Daniels Estate, p. 26.

The influence of Coach Babe Godfrey: "Bill Daniels: The Father of Cable TV" oral history interview by Max Paglin, conducted February 10, 1986, for The Cable Center's Hauser Oral and Video History Collection.

Bill made friends easily and enjoyed getting to know young men from all over the country: Letter from Bill to Major Alfred L. Castle, NMMI, August 26, 1983.

As he developed discipline, he learned how to discipline others, and he gradually became a leader: Letter from Bill to Cadet Cameron Gray, New Mexico Military Institute, August 17, 1989.

Second chances story: Bill Daniels' acceptance speech for Will Rogers Memorial Award, NMMI, undated.

Oilfield pipelining: Mohler, J. C. "A Biography: This Is Bill Daniels." Publication unknown, circa 1974.

Bill would rather be a fighter pilot than take care of a horse: Letter from Bill to Howard G. Klein, San Antonio, April 29, 1998.

Chapter Four

Opening quote — "People say to me that I am a real hero . . .": Letter from Bill to Bob Delbridge, October 30, 1998.

Bill's Naval flight training history: Mohler, J. C. "A Biography: This Is Bill Daniels." Publication unknown, circa 1974.

Bill earns $187.50 / "I had never seen so much money": Letter from Bill to Bob Delbridge, October 30, 1998.

Planes Bill flew: Letter from Bill to Ken Clute, May 13, 1984.

Bill's World War II battle history: Tribute to "Robert William Daniels" at the Sea-Air Operations Exhibition, Smithsonian National Air and Space Museum, www.nasm.si.edu/exhibitions/gal203/daniels.cfm; "Bill Daniels: The Father of Cable TV" oral history interview by Max Paglin, conducted February 10, 1986, for The Cable Center's Hauser Oral and Video History Collection; Letter from Bill to Howard G. Klein, San Antonio, April 29, 1998; Letter from Bill to Ken Clute, May 13, 1984.

Night-fighter experience: Two letters from Bill to Ken Clute, May 13, 1984, and July 25, 1994.

Story of trading planes: Letter from Bill to Donal Broesamle, October 21, 1997.

Bill was sent to "fighter director school" in St. Simons Island, Georgia: "Bill Daniels: The Father of Cable TV" oral history interview by Max Paglin, conducted February 10, 1986, for The Cable Center's Hauser Oral and Video History Collection.

Bill participated in Battle of Leyte Gulf: Letter from Bill to Ken Clute, May 13, 1984.

World War II service history of the U.S.S. *Intrepid*: www. en.wikipedia.org/wiki/USS_Intrepid_(CV-11).

Shoving fighter planes overboard: Two letters from Bill to Ken Clute, May 13, 1984, and July 25, 1994.

Bill's experience of *kamikaze* attack on U.S.S. *Intrepid*: Letter from Bill to Bill O'Brien, December 9, 1994; Maxwell, Paul. "Bill Daniels: First of the Pioneers…And Still Crusading." *Denver Business World*, December 11, 1978.

Bill served under admirals Nimitz and Halsey: Letter from Bill to Ken Clute, May 13, 1994.

The US Navy awarded Daniels the Air Medal: Tribute to "Robert William Daniels" at the Sea-Air Operations Exhibition, Smithsonian National Air and Space Museum: www.nasm.si.edu/exhibitions/gal203/daniels.cfm.

Ferrying fighter aircraft from Brooklyn to San Diego: "Bill Daniels: The Father of Cable TV" oral history interview by Max Paglin, conducted February 10, 1986, for The Cable Center's Hauser Oral and Video History Collection.

"I really liked living the Navy life": Letter from Bill to Howard G. Klein, San Antonio, April 29, 1998.

"I went through one tough period . . .": Letter from Bill to Wayne Harding, Denver, September 17, 1987.

"The Chaplain used to tell us . . .": Letter from Bill to Bob Delbridge, February 18, 1999.

Bill kept a picture of one of the planes he flew: Letter from Bill to Richard Deihl, H. F. Ahmanson & Co., Los Angeles, April 24, 1987.

"It rubbed off on me . . .": *Tom Kelly Interviews Bill Daniels*. DVD. June 15, 1990.

Bill's mother hoped he'd become a doctor: Letter from Bill to Letitia Baldrige, May 7, 1997.

Rejoining insurance business and Bill's dad's death: Singular, Stephen. (2003). *Relentless: Bill Daniels and the Triumph of Cable TV*. The Bill Daniels Estate, p. 39; Letter from Bill to Bob Delbridge, July 1, 1998.

"I wasn't doing what I wanted to do" and "Nothing better than being a fighter pilot": Letter from Bill to Cameron Gray, January 25, 2000.

"What am I doin' way out here again?": Mohler, J. C. "A Biography: This Is Bill Daniels." Publication unknown, circa 1974.

Chapter Five

Opening quote — "If there is any reason . . .": "Bill Daniels: The Father of Cable TV" oral history interview by Max Paglin, conducted February 10, 1986, for The Cable Center's Hauser Oral and Video History Collection.

"You never know when a sweet deal is going to walk in the door" and story about notarizing papers: Bill's speech to Dartmouth College students, 1986.

Bill leaves the insurance business to his brother: Letter from Bill to Donal Broesamle, October 7, 1998.

He drove all over the Rocky Mountain area: "Bill Daniels: The Father of Cable TV" oral history interview by Max Paglin, conducted February 10, 1986, for The Cable Center's Hauser Oral and Video History Collection.

Murphy's Bar: Smith, Brad. "Bill Daniels: The Life and Times of the King of Cable." *Colorado Business*, August 1994.

Bill is impressed by the invention of TV / "I couldn't get it out of my mind": "Bill Daniels: The Father of Cable TV" oral history interview by Max Paglin, conducted February 10, 1986, for The Cable Center's Hauser Oral and Video History Collection.

History of cable TV invention prior to Bill, and Bill's Casper experiment: Singular, Stephen. (2003). *Relentless: Bill Daniels and the Triumph of Cable TV*. The Bill Daniels Estate, pp. 44-56; "Bill Daniels: The Father of Cable TV" oral history interview by Max Paglin, conducted February 10, 1986, for The Cable Center's Hauser Oral and Video History Collection.

"It was tough raising money": Mohler, J. C. "A Biography: This Is Bill Daniels." Publication unknown, circa 1974.

"I knew we were going to have a wired nation one day": Smith, Brad. "Bill Daniels: The Life and Times of the King of Cable." *Colorado Business*, August 1994.

"The Father of Cable Television": "Bill Daniels: The Father of Cable TV" oral history interview by Max Paglin, conducted February 10, 1986, for The Cable Center's Hauser Oral and Video History Collection.

Chapter Six

Opening quote — "A person's integrity . . .": Letter from Bill to Marc Weisberg, April 4, 1997.

"I hope they would say . . .": Smith, Brad. "Bill Daniels: The Life and Times of the King of Cable. *Colorado Business*, August 1994.

Bill remembers walking the halls of the House and Senate: Letter from Bill to Senator Hank Brown, US Senator from Colorado, July 8, 1991.

". . . we must have something. If we didn't, they could care less about us": Bill's speech to Dartmouth College students, 1986.

Bill saw it as a classic case of the free enterprise system at its best: Letter from Bill to Senator Hank Brown, US Senator from Colorado, July 8, 1991.

Bill starts matching buyers and sellers and then founds Daniels & Associates: "Daniels & Associates 25th Anniversary," *Cablevision*, 2(27), July 25, 1983.

Charles A. Sammons: Bill's speech to Dartmouth College students, 1986.

Bill stops to talk to the janitors at City Hall while waiting for a meeting with the mayor: *Daniels Fund Directors Remember Bill Daniels*. DVD. Denver: Daniels Fund, 2010.

"Neither a scrooge nor a patsy be": Bill's speech to Dartmouth College students, 1986.

Bill's Learjet: Singular, Stephen. "Wired for Success: Denver's Cable King Bill Daniels Knows What Makes Television Work — Money." *Empire Magazine* of the *Denver Post*, March 20, 1983.

"I love work": Mohler, J. C. "A Biography: This Is Bill Daniels." Publication unknown, circa 1974.

His systems were praised . . .: "Biographical Profile: Bill Daniels" (an undated media piece produced by Bill's company).

"Once the deal is put together . . .": "Daniels & Associates 25th Anniversary," *Cablevision*, 2(27), July 25, 1983.

"Every decision he ever made . . .": Singular, Stephen. (2003). *Relentless: Bill Daniels and the Triumph of Cable TV*. The Bill Daniels Estate, p. 180.

Index cards: *A Matter of Courage*. DVD. Denver: Produced by Dewey-Obenchain Films, May 31, 2002.

"I would leave town on Christmas day": Salmans, Sandra. "The Cable Industry's No. 1 Deal Maker." *The New York Times*, October 16, 1983.

"My business always came before my love affairs": Bill's speech to Dartmouth College students, 1986.

"I was more interested in my business": Letter from Bill to Cameron Gray, January 25, 2000.

Bill jokes that he would want to be reincarnated as one of his ex-wives: Interview with Ed Beck, September 2009.

Chapter Seven

Opening quote — "You will find this company one of the easiest ones to work for . . .": Bill's "Memo to All Associates," April 7, 1982.

John Saeman and "The way I measure success . . .": "Daniels & Associates 25th Anniversary," *Cablevision*, 2(27), July 25, 1983.

"I've always told people they don't work for me . . ." and "People want more than a paycheck": *The Future Begins Here*. DVD. Denver: Young Americans Education Foundation, digitized 2010.

Bill was "the most trusting person": *Daniels Fund Directors Remember Bill Daniels*. DVD. Denver: Daniels Fund, 2010.

". . . to hell with the stock . . .": Letter from Bill to Captain Charles Conrad, January 7, 1970.

Bill's involvement with Ted Turner and CNN: Letter from Bill to Bob Delbridge, April 4, 1997.

Bill invested in mobile communications: Symonds, William C. " 'Wild Bill' Daniels Tries One More Comeback.' " *Business Week*, January 30, 1989.

Prime Ticket: "Biographical Profile: Bill Daniels" (an undated media piece produced by Bill's company).

Tony Acone is president of Prime Ticket: Stewart, Larry. "New President of Prime Ticket Named." *Los Angeles Times*, September 9, 1988, articles.latimes.com/1988-09-09/sports/sp-1893_1_prime-ticket.

Bill asks Tony Acone to investigate feasibility of regional sports network: *Daniels Fund Directors Remember Bill Daniels*. DVD. Denver: Daniels Fund, 2010.

Bill merged 24 of his cable systems with United Artists Communications: Smith, Brad. "Bill Daniels: The Life and Times of the King of Cable." *Colorado Business*, August 1994.

"I've tried to share throughout my career": Romano, Michael. "Bill Daniels Does Encore." Rocky Mountain News, September 2, 1988.

"There is only one way to do things, and that is first class": Letter from Bill to David and Agnes Palmer, January 5, 1970.

"The best is good enough for me": Singular, Stephen. "Wired for Success: Denver's Cable King Bill Daniels Knows What Makes Television Work — Money." *Empire Magazine* of the *Denver Post*, March 20, 1983.

"Dress properly within your budget": *Bill Daniels on "The Real World of Business"*. DVD. Casper, Wyoming: Casper College, October 6, 1992.

Bill is a "stickler for neatness and well organized desks": Letter from Bill to Richard D. Barron, December 5, 1989.

"I have spent more money per square foot . . .": undated memo from Bill to "All Denver Associates."

Quick dismantling of fishpond: Singular, Stephen. (2003). *Relentless: Bill Daniels and the Triumph of Cable TV*. The Bill Daniels Estate, pp. 89-90.

Reward to driver of clean cable truck: Singular, Stephen. (2003). *Relentless: Bill Daniels and the Triumph of Cable TV*. The Bill Daniels Estate, p. 90.

"When you talk with him, it's like speaking with your career counselor": Singular, Stephen. "Wired for Success: Denver's Cable King Bill Daniels Knows What Makes Television Work — Money." *Empire Magazine* of the *Denver Post*, March 20, 1983.

Bill's battle with alcoholism: Singular, Stephen. (2003). *Relentless: Bill Daniels and the Triumph of Cable TV*. The Bill Daniels Estate, pp. 273-276; Smith, Brad. "Bill Daniels: The Life and Times of the King of Cable." *Colorado Business*, August 1994.

Chapter Eight

Opening quote — "I fought in two wars . . .": Letter from Bill to Congressman Randy "Duke" Cunningham, Washington, D.C., September 4, 1992.

Politics is participation in government: Bill's Arizona CATV Assoc. Speech. "Bill Daniels' address to Arizona Community Access Television". DVD. Denver: Daniels Fund, 1986.

Why Bill ran for governor: Letter from Bill to "Fellow Republicans," September 1974.

Bill traveled to every county in the state: Letter from Bill to Dan Green, Editor, The Record Stockman, Wheatridge, Colorado, December 10, 1997.

"I have always felt we should have more businessmen in government" and "It's a blessing in disguise that I wasn't elected": "Daniels & Associates 25th Anniversary," *Cablevision*, 2(27), July 25, 1983.

Cable industry is free enterprise system at its best: Letter from Bill to Senator Hank Brown, July 8, 1991

Cable industry's impact on U.S. economy: "Biographical Profile: Bill Daniels" (an undated media piece produced by Bill's company).

"I'm very proud of Young Americans Bank . . .": from Bill's Cable TV Hall of Fame acceptance speech, 1998.

Chapter Nine

Opening Quote — "It's all fun . . .": *Making Life Better . . . One Individual at a Time*. DVD. Denver. Daniels Fund, 2006.

Bill prays for Lakers win: Letter from Bill to Monsignor C. B. Woodrich, Holy Ghost Catholic Church, Denver, June 23, 1988.

Father Woody known as "Denver's Patron Saint of the Poor": www.FatherWoody.org.

Bill called his sports enterprises "charities": Singular, Stephen. "Wired for Success: Denver's Cable King Bill Daniels Knows What Makes Television Work — Money." *Empire Magazine* of the *Denver Post*, March 20, 1983.

Bill visits prisons as YPO activity and talks about his partnership with boxers: Mohler, J. C. "A Biography: This Is Bill Daniels." Publication unknown, circa 1974.

Lyle fights Ali and then leaves Daniels: Maxwell, Paul. "Bill Daniels: First of the Pioneers…and Still Crusading." Publication unknown; Singular, Stephen. "Wired for Success: Denver's Cable King Bill Daniels Knows What Makes Television Work — Money." *Empire Magazine* of the *Denver Post*, March 20, 1983; Singular, Stephen. (2003). *Relentless: Bill Daniels and the Triumph of Cable TV*. The Bill Daniels Estate, p. 170.

Utah Stars: *Bill Daniels on "The Real World of Business"*. DVD. Casper, Wyoming: Casper College, October 6, 1992; Singular, Stephen. "Wired for Success: Denver's Cable King Bill Daniels Knows What Makes Television Work — Money." *Empire Magazine* of the *Denver Post*, March 20, 1983.

USFL: *Daniels Fund Directors Remember Bill Daniels*. DVD. Denver: Daniels Fund, 2010.

Lost $200,000 sponsoring Indy 500 driver: Singular, Stephen. "Wired for Success: Denver's Cable King Bill Daniels Knows What Makes Television Work — Money." *Empire Magazine* of the *Denver Post*, March 20, 1983.

". . . I had a ball": Letter from Bill to Gene Clark, January 21, 1981.

". . . how crazy sports ownership is": Letter from Bill to Bob Delbridge, June 17, 1998.

Denver Grand Prix: Daniels Fund website; Smith, Brad. "Bill Daniels: The Life and Times of the King of Cable." *Colorado Business*, August 1994.

Bill prevented damage to Denver's fledging reputation: Daniels Fund Ethics Initiative brochure, p. 2.

Chapter Ten

Opening quote — "I ask my fellow . . .": Letter from Bill to Dan Ritchie and Dwight Smith, Chancellor, University of Denver, August 16, 1988.

Address to Atlantic Cable Show: Daniels, Bill. "Cable Cares." *CableVision*, October 23, 1989.

"Cable Cares" study: "Biographical Profile: Bill Daniels" (an undated media piece produced by Bill's company).

Bill's generosity to families in immediate need, homeless shelters, food pantries: Accola, John. "Larger Than Life: Reflections on an Extraordinary Man and His Legacy." *Rocky Mountain News*, March 12, 2000; *A Matter of Courage*. DVD. Denver: Produced by Dewey-Obenchain Films, May 31, 2002; Interview with Ed Beck, September, 2009.

Bill's support of his sister Dorothy and the institution that cared for her: *Daniels Fund Directors Remember Bill Daniels*. DVD. Denver: Daniels Fund, 2010; Letter from Bill to Bob Gutkowski with check for "Adults / Children with Learning Disabilities," June 1, 1993.

Dorothy Daniels' death date and age: www.faqs.org/people-search/daniels-new-mexico/ - "Dorothy Daniels, born: March 27, 1919, died: May 1, 1986, 67 years, NM 88240, Hobbs, Lea County."

Adele Daniels' death date and age: findagrave.com.

Bill's support of amateur athletes: Singular, Stephen. *Relentless: Bill Daniels and the Triumph of Cable TV*. The Bill Daniels Estate, p. 248-249; Letter from Bill to Jack Fenlon, Aurora, Colorado, September 18, 1987.

Bill's support of NMMI students: Letter from Bill to Cameron Gray, January 13, 1992.

"There is virtually no place in the country . . .": Letter from Bill to Ambassador Walter Annenberg, November 28, 1988.

". . . business is people": Letter from Bill to Dan Ritchie and Dwight Smith, Chancellor, University of Denver, August 16, 1988.

Cableland dispute with neighbors: Smith, Brad. "Bill Daniels: The Life and Times of the King of Cable." *Colorado Business*, August 1994.

Chapter Eleven

Opening quote — "I say my . . .": Letter from Bill to Mr. and Mrs. W. H. Reeves, Brevard, North Carolina, August 14, 1986.

Aluminum cross: Letter from Bill to Dan Donahue, James Watson, and Brian Lawrence, December 24, 1995.

Bill gives cross to Jewish gentleman, meets Reverend Ed Beck: Interview with Ed Beck, September, 2009.

Faith in God helped Bill stay sober: Letter from Bill to Wayne Harding, Denver, September 17, 1987.

"I have a severe hearing problem": *Bill Daniels on "The Real World of Business"*. DVD. Casper, Wyoming: Casper College, October 6, 1992.

Diverticulitis and near death experience: Communications between the Daniels Fund and Mark Calkins, 2011.

"I say my prayers . . .": Letter from Bill to Mr. and Mrs. W. H. Reeves, Brevard, North Carolina, August 14, 1986.

"Not only have I been lucky . . .": Letter from Bill to Pat Tinley, January 25, 2000.

Lighted cross: *Daniels Fund Directors Remember Bill Daniels*. DVD. Denver: Daniels Fund, 2010.

Bill asks Mark Calkins about his faith: Communications between the Daniels Fund and Mark Calkins, 2011.

Bill and Reverend Beck discuss the "borrowed time" Bill received to finish setting up his foundation: Interview with Ed Beck, September, 2009.

Gerald Ford's tribute to Bill: Video of Bill's Roast, July 7, 1987 — "Lifestyles of the Rich and Famous" (approximately 22:04).

Chapter Twelve

Opening quote — "I spend most . . .": Letter from Bill to Lt. General Robert Beckel, USAF, Roswell, New Mexico, October 6, 1999.

Suggestion for *Forbes* magazine: Letter from Bill to Malcolm S. Forbes Jr., April 24, 1995.

One of Bill's friends dies without a well-designed estate plan: Hofmeister, Sallie. "TCI, Late Founder's Family Settle Legal Dispute." *Los Angeles Times*, January 6, 1998.

The four states "contributed to the luck I have had": Letter from Bill to Frederick R. Mayer, Denver, February 18, 1999.

"Please remember that I am a conservative": Letter from Bill to the Board of Directors of the Daniels Foundation, July 29, 1998.

Bill believed in conservative Republican tenets: Letter from Bill to "Fellow Republicans" about his run for governor, 1974; and "Memorandum from Bill Daniels," November, 20, 1973.

"Most of my giving just does not match with symphonies, art, and opera": Letter from Bill to Frederick R. Mayer, Denver, February 18, 1999.

Comments from Linda Childears and John Saeman about the early challenges of operationalizing donor intent: Sparks, Evan. "Back to Bill: How the Daniels Fund Lost Sight of Bill Daniels, Clawed Its Way Back . . ." *Philanthropy Magazine*, Fall 2011.

"I think God told me as a young man . . .": Letter from Bill to Bill McGorry, September 16, 1999.

Chapter Thirteen

Opening quote — "If you've never taken a chance on yourself . . .": Daniels Fund Scholarship Program brochure, cover.

Bill's expectations when paying for college: Letter from Bill to Cameron Gray, January 13, 1992.

"I enjoy sharing my good fortune . . .": Letter from Bill to Carol Roderick, June 2, 1992.

"I had zilch formal education": *Bill Daniels on "The Real World of Business"*. DVD. Casper, Wyoming: Casper College, October 6, 1992.

"I never had an accounting course" and story about quid pro quo: Bill's speech to Dartmouth College students, 1986.

". . . four letters from alumni . . .": Letter from Bill to John Saeman, March 14, 1997.

"He had an innate ability . . .": *Daniels Fund Directors Remember Bill Daniels*. DVD. Denver: Daniels Fund, 2010.

"Bill Daniels just loved young people.": *Daniels Fund Directors Remember Bill Daniels*. DVD. Denver: Daniels Fund, 2010.

"When these kids graduate . . .": Singular, Stephen. (2003). *Relentless: Bill Daniels and the Triumph of Cable TV*. The Bill Daniels Estate, p. 288. (Note: these sentences have been reordered from how they were quoted in book.)

Chapter Fourteen

Opening quote — "My greatest hero was my mother. . .": Letter from Bill to Cameron Gray, January 25, 2000.

Adele held her family together: Singular, Stephen. (2003). *Relentless: Bill Daniels and the Triumph of Cable TV*. The Bill Daniels Estate, p, 139.

Adele doesn't go to every one of Bill's weddings: Singular, Stephen. (2003). *Relentless: Bill Daniels and the Triumph of Cable TV*. The Bill Daniels Estate, p. 136.

Bill interrupts his dates to call his mother: Singular, Stephen. (2003). *Relentless: Bill Daniels and the Triumph of Cable TV*. The Bill Daniels Estate, pp. 138-139.

Bill calls his mom when he gets Denver cable contract: "25 Who Count: Bill Daniels." *Inside View: The Magazine of Television Programming*, 4(11), November 1983.

Adele Daniels' death date and age: findagrave.com.

Mother's Day is tough day for Bill: Letter from Bill to Margolyn Woods, November 22, 1999.

Gift to waitress in Christmas card: Singular, Stephen. *Relentless: Bill Daniels and the Triumph of Cable TV*. The Bill Daniels Estate p. 42.

". . . pay a visit to an elderly neighbor": Advertisements produced by the Daniels Fund on Bill's Philosophies, 1980s.

Letter to elderly friend in nursing home: Letter from Bill to Leah Christensen, Cedars, Lakewood, Colorado, January 8, 1987.

Bill's 1996 emergency surgery and aftermath: Various 1997 letters from Bill to friends.

Reversing colostomy: Singular, Stephen. (2003). *Relentless: Bill Daniels and the Triumph of Cable TV*. The Bill Daniels Estate, p. 310.

Settled back at beach house: Various 1997 letters from Bill to friends.

Bill can't breathe in high-altitude Denver: Accola, John. "Larger Than Life: Reflections on an Extraordinary Man and His Legacy." *Rocky Mountain News*, March 12, 2000.

Bill's nurse, housekeeper, and secretary: Singular, Stephen. (2003). *Relentless: Bill Daniels and the Triumph of Cable TV*. The Bill Daniels Estate, p. 308.

Bill tells Broe he is "down in the dumps": Letter from Bill to Donal Broesamle, August 19, 1997.

Frank Sinatra quotes: Letter from Bill to Bob Delbridge, June 17, 1998.

". . . pissed off that I am old": Letter from Bill to Kate Burnett, July 8, 1998.

"Screw the golden years!" pillow: Letter from Bill to Letitia Baldrige, September 16, 1999.

Bill feels like a "prisoner": Letter from Bill to Margolyn Woods, November 22, 1999.

Bill "can't complain": Letter from Bill to Letitia Baldrige, September 16, 1999.

Bill believes God saved him in 1996 so he could do more good: Letter from Bill to Hap and Doris Reeves, September 23, 1997.

Chapter Fifteen

Opening quote — "If you're gonna gamble . . .": *Daniels Fund Directors Remember Bill Daniels*. DVD. Denver: Daniels Fund, 2010.

Bill left Betty Ford Center on May 14, 1985: Letter from Bill to Jerry Buss, June 7, 1985.

In jail for drunk driving: Bill's speech to Dartmouth College students, 1986.

Bill's March 1985 bender, help from friends, and experience at Betty Ford Center: Singular, Stephen. (2003). *Relentless: Bill Daniels and the Triumph of Cable TV*. The Bill Daniels Estate, pp. 273-276.

"I made up my mind that I had too many things left in my lifetime to let alcohol get the best of me": Bill's speech to Dartmouth College students, 1986.

Bill's father was an alcoholic: "Bill Daniels: The Father of Cable TV" oral history interview by Max Paglin, conducted February 10, 1986, for The Cable Center's Hauser Oral and Video History Collection.

Bill's sister had a drinking problem: *Daniels Fund Directors Remember Bill Daniels*. DVD. Denver: Daniels Fund, 2010.

Open letter to associates about his drinking problem: Smith, Brad. "Bill Daniels: The Life and Times of the King of Cable." *Colorado Business*, August 1994.

Jerry Buss: Letter from Bill to Jerry Buss, June 7, 1985.

"January 2 will be nine months since I've had a drink . . .": Letter to Rupert Dunklau, December 23, 1985.

"I enjoy giving people a second chance": Letter from Bill to Douglass Gerash, May 4, 1993.

Letter to friend who was in jail with DUI: Letter from Bill to "Jack," October, 10, 1988.

First alumnus to serve on the Betty Ford Center board: Letter from Bill to Ambassador Walter Annenberg, August 10, 1988.

Quote from Betty Ford: *A Matter of Courage*. DVD. Denver: Produced by Dewey-Obenchain Films, May 31, 2002.

Letter to Betty Ford Center associates: Letter from Bill to Betty Ford Center, December 16, 1985.

Chapter Sixteen

Opening quote — "If you didn't mow the lawn . . .": Advertisements produced by the Daniels Fund on Bill's Philosophies, 1980s.

Bob Daniels sends Bill to military school: Singular, Stephen. (2003). *Relentless: Bill Daniels and the Triumph of Cable TV*. The Bill Daniels Estate, p. 25.

Coach Storm and Bill's football record: Letter from Bill to Ann S. Lane, Black Forest, Colorado, August 2, 1995.

Bill letters in football and leads an undefeated basketball team: Singular, Stephen. (2003). *Relentless: Bill Daniels and the Triumph of Cable TV*. The Bill Daniels Estate, p. 27.

Coach Godfrey calls Bill "Jeep": Singular, Stephen. (2003). *Relentless: Bill Daniels and the Triumph of Cable TV*. The Bill Daniels Estate, p. 26.

Principles learned from Coach Godfrey and Bill is grateful: "Bill Daniels: The Father of Cable TV" oral history interview by Max Paglin, conducted February 10, 1986, for The Cable Center's Hauser Oral and Video History Collection.

Bill's Golden Gloves career: Smith, Brad. "Bill Daniels: The Life and Times of the King of Cable." *Colorado Business*, August 1994; *Tom Kelly Interviews Bill Daniels*. DVD. June 15, 1990.

The first television show Bill saw was a boxing match: Smith, Brad. "Bill Daniels: The Life and Times of the King of Cable." *Colorado Business*, August 1994.

Boxing is favorite sport: Letter from Bill to Donal Broesamle, August 19, 1997.

Denver Boxing Club: Mohler, J. C. "A Biography: This Is Bill Daniels." Publication unknown, circa 1974.

Denver Rocks: Singular, Stephen. (2003). *Relentless: Bill Daniels and the Triumph of Cable TV*. The Bill Daniels Estate, p. 169.

Bill brought fighters from New York to Denver: Mohler, J. C. "A Biography: This Is Bill Daniels." Publication unknown, circa 1974.

"More club owners . . . ": Quoted from a 1973 newspaper article "Daniels & Associates 25th Anniversary" in *Cablevision*, 2(27), July 25, 1983.

Scott Hamilton info and quotes: Singular, Stephen. (2003). *Relentless: Bill Daniels and the Triumph of Cable TV*. The Bill Daniels Estate, p. 248-249.

Allyson Fenlon contribution: Letter from Bill to Jack Fenlon, Aurora, Colorado, September 18, 1987.

Bryan Pattison recommendation: Letter from Bill to James Griesemer, dean of Daniels College of Business, asking Jim to forward it to the dean of the Law School, September 16, 1996.

Roger Staubach: Letter from Bill to Roger Staubach, Dallas, May 4, 1999.

Chapter Seventeen

Opening quote — "Everybody is important to me": Letter from Bill to Bruce Heverly, August 18, 1994.

Jimmy Carroll, blind piano player in mall: Letter from Bill to the manager of La Jolla Village Square, La Jolla, California, October 27, 1981.

Sister Dorothy and remembrances of "Aunt Dotty": *Daniels Fund Directors Remember Bill Daniels*. DVD. Denver: Daniels Fund, 2010.

Dorothy Daniels' death date: www.faqs.org/people-search/daniels-new-mexico/ - "Dorothy Daniels, born: March 27, 1919, died: May 1, 1986, 67 years, New Mexico 88240, Hobbs, Lea County."

Adele Daniels' death date: www.findagrave.com.

Bill honored his sister with ongoing financial support to the facility: Letter from Bill to Bob Gutkowski with check for "Adults / Children with Learning Disabilities," June 1, 1993.

Development of hearing loss: Letter from Bill to Bonnie Means, February 20, 1992.

Bill tells his great-nephew to get his hearing checked: Letter from Bill to Spencer Schreiber, undated.

Bill tells Broe he is struggling with hearing loss: Letter from Bill to Donal Broesamle, June 17, 1993.

Chapter Eighteen

Opening quote — "Quality education for all should be our goal": Daniels, Bill. Statement of his position on issues during his campaign for Governor of Colorado, April 7, 1974, unpublished document.

Encouraging Will McGorry to do well in school: Letter from Bill to Pam and Will Tully, January 27, 2000.

Bill compliments his closest associates for their parenting: Letter from Bill to John and Carol Saeman, March 14, 1997; Letter from Bill to John Saeman, February 9, 1994.

Associates bragged to Bill about their children's achievements: Letter from Bill to John Schonewill, Sachs Communications, Englewood, Colorado, January 14, 1991.

Letter of praise for straight As: Letter from Bill to Lisa Benton, November 30, 1994.

Chapter Nineteen

Opening quote — "I am a great believer . . .": Letter from Bill to Debe Allen, Oklahoma, September 1, 1993.

Bill at school's parents' night: Singular, Stephen. (2003). *Relentless: Bill Daniels and the Triumph of Cable TV*. The Bill Daniels Estate, pp. 252-253.

NMMI taught practical skills: "Bill Daniels: The Father of Cable TV" oral history interview by Max Paglin, conducted February 10, 1986, for The Cable Center's Hauser Oral and Video History Collection.

"An entrepreneur dealing with the academic community": Letter from Bill to David Ferguson, Denver, May 4, 1993.

People over 60 felt they received a better education: Letter from Bill to Debe Allen, Oklahoma, September 1, 1993.

Poor education diminishes global competitiveness: Linda Childears and Kim Dennis. Philanthropy Roundtable presentation, October 16, 2010.

Likes school voucher program in Michigan: Letter from Bill to Debe Allen, Oklahoma, September 1, 1993.

Support for Colorado amendment: Memo from Bill to "All Denver Associates" about Amendment 17, October 14, 1998.

Merrill Middle School project with jet flight: Letter from Bill to Susan Poutre, Assistant Principal, Merrill Middle School, Denver, February 21, 1996.

Chapter Twenty

Opening quote — "I'm hopeful that my investment in ethics education . . .": Letter from Bill to Edward Conry, Professor of Business Law and Ethics, University of Colorado at Denver, January 3, 1989.

Bill cries in hotel room about Utah Stars and talks to lawyer: *Bill Daniels on "The Real World of Business"*. DVD. Casper, Wyoming: Casper College, October 6, 1992.

Bill lost $5 million on Utah Stars: Singular, Stephen. "Wired for Success: Denver's Cable King Bill Daniels Knows What Makes Television Work — Money." *Empire Magazine* of the *Denver Post*, March 20, 1983.

"I had to look myself in the mirror . . .": *Bill Daniels on "The Real World of Business"*. DVD. Casper, Wyoming: Casper College, October 6, 1992.

"I want to leave the face of the earth with a good reputation . . .": Singular, Stephen. "Wired for Success: Denver's Cable King Bill Daniels Knows What Makes Television Work — Money." *Empire Magazine* of the *Denver Post*, March 20, 1983.

Bill waits to start his company until after he is done being president of trade association: Bill's speech to Dartmouth College students, 1986.

"The numbers are often secondary": Maxwell, Paul. "Bill Daniels: First of the Pioneers...and Still Crusading." Publication unknown.

"They have a real reputation for square dealing . . .": Clayton, Kathy. "Daniels' Winning Method." *Electronic Media*, August 21, 1989.

"The integrity of this firm means more to me than dollars": Letter from Bill to Bob Gould, Anchorage, Alaska, May 23, 1985.

Bill fired associates for lying: "Understanding the Man Behind the Daniels Fund," May 2008.

Bill scolds young colleague in a letter about living up to his commitments: Letter from Bill to private individual; Lawrence, Kansas, July 10, 1984.

Bill learns that no business schools teach ethics: *Bill Daniels on "The Real World of Business"*. DVD. Casper, Wyoming: Casper College, October 6, 1992.

"Integrity in business is the ultimate competitive advantage": "Understanding the Man Behind the Daniels Fund," May 2008, attributed to "BD commenting on a quote from the CEO of Coke, August 11, 1998."

List of lessons expected to be taught to Denver University business students: Memo from Bill to Phil Hogue, May 17, 1989.

Bill talking at DU renaming ceremony: Berenson, Alex. "DU renames school for Daniels." *The Denver Post*, September 14, 1994.

Chapter Twenty-One

Opening quote — "I am for the underdog": Letter from Bill to Frederick R. Mayer, Denver, February 18, 1999.

Bill helps homeless shelter for addicted men: Letter from Bill to Step 13 Evolution Process Inc., November 20, 1985.

"Those of us more fortunate than others . . .": Letter from Bill to Father John V. Anderson, Director of Major Giving, Samaritan House Fund, February 18, 1987.

"My brother and I used to gather firewood...": "Bill Daniels: The Father of Cable TV" oral history interview by Max Paglin, conducted February 10, 1986, for The Cable Center's Hauser Oral and Video History Collection.

"I believe in working hard . . .": Mohler, J. C. "A Biography: This Is Bill Daniels." Publication unknown, circa 1974.

"Pick yourself up . . ." pet rock: Accola, John. "Larger Than Life: Reflections on an Extraordinary Man and His Legacy." *Rocky Mountain News*, March 12, 2000.

Bill and Phil Hogue go to Father Woody's meal for the hungry: Accola, John. "Larger Than Life: Reflections on an Extraordinary Man and His Legacy." *Rocky Mountain News*, March 12, 2000.

"The joy of my life today . . .": Letter from Bill to Bob Delbridge, November 30, 1999.

Organ transplant donations: "Daniels & Associates 25th Anniversary," *Cablevision*, 2(27), July 25, 1983.

"I think he was more touched by people he read about": Singular, Stephen. (2003). *Relentless: Bill Daniels and the Triumph of Cable TV*. The Bill Daniels Estate, p. 256.

"My airplane is available to fly severely injured or ill people": Letter from Bill to Barry Hirschfeld, August 2, 1993.

Bill gives away his Cadillac: Clayton, Kathy. "Daniels' Winning Method." *Electronic Media*, August 21, 1989.

Bill gives to salesman from Salt Lake City: Accola, John. "Larger Than Life: Reflections on an Extraordinary Man and His Legacy." *Rocky Mountain News*, March 12, 2000.

Big tips to waitstaff: *Daniels Fund Directors Remember Bill Daniels*. DVD. Denver: Daniels Fund, 2010.

Bill offers to lend June Travis money for a new house: *Daniels Fund Directors Remember Bill Daniels*. DVD. Denver: Daniels Fund, 2010.

"I realize from time to time . . .": Letter from Bill to Board of Directors of the Daniels Foundation, March 3, 1998.

Chapter Twenty-Two

Opening quote — "I have supported young people all my life": Letter from Bill to Carol Roderick, June 2, 1992.

Daniels family during Depression: Singular, Stephen. (2003). *Relentless: Bill Daniels and the Triumph of Cable TV*. The Bill Daniels Estate, pp. 22-23.

Early jobs and Bill's quotes about selling ice cream and working to survive: "Bill Daniels: The Father of Cable TV" oral history interview by Max Paglin, conducted February 10, 1986, for The Cable Center's Hauser Oral and Video History Collection.

Working as a bellboy: Letter from Bill to Bob Delbridge, October 30, 1998.

Learning in military school and Navy: "Bill Daniels: The Father of Cable TV" oral history interview by Max Paglin, conducted February 10, 1986, for The Cable Center's Hauser Oral and Video History Collection.

Students are expected to report monthly to Bill on their grades, etc.: Letter from Bill to Cameron Gray, January 13, 1992.

Quote from Jim Griesemer: *Daniels Fund Directors Remember Bill Daniels*. DVD. Denver: Daniels Fund, 2010.

Bill forgot to send thank-you note: Letter from Bill to Michael Thompson, March 29, 1994.

Hoang Nhu Tran: Advertisements produced by the Daniels Fund on Bill's Philosophies, 1980s.

Chapter Twenty-Three

Opening quote — "I have always felt the best way to teach kids about money management . . .": Letter from Bill to "Friends & Associates" involved with Young Americans Bank, January 21, 1994.

Bill was intimidated by banks: "Bill Daniels' Thoughts on Linda and Phil Going to Russia," unpublished document, 1995.

Newspaper article about fifth-grade class wanting a bank loan: *A Matter of Courage*. DVD. Denver: Produced by Dewey-Obenchain Films, May 31, 2002.

"It doesn't take a rocket scientist . . .": "Bill Daniels' Thoughts on Linda and Phil Going to Russia," unpublished document, 1995.

"I want our bank to show kids how to conduct everyday banking transactions . . .": Letter from Bill to Robert L. Clarke, Comptroller of the Currency, Washington, D.C., September 16, 1986.

Bill's vision for the bank and overcoming regulatory hurdles: Interview with Linda Childears, November 3, 2011; "Young Americans Policy," August 2009, Daniels Fund unpublished document; Childears, Linda. "The Evolution of Young Americans and the Vision of Its Founder, Bill Daniels," October 5, 2010, presentation.

Banking climate in the mid-1980s: Interview with Linda Childears, November 3, 2011.

"Most banks don't want to talk to their regulators": Interview with Linda Childears, November 3, 2011.

Bill tells Linda Childears to fix whatever problems she encountered: Singular, Stephen. (2003). *Relentless: Bill Daniels and the Triumph of Cable TV*. The Bill Daniels Estate, p. 290.

Getting stores to accept Young Americans Bank's checks: Childears, Linda. "The Evolution of Young Americans and the Vision of Its Founder, Bill Daniels," October 25, 2010, presentation.

Description of bank opening through to 8,000 accounts by the second year: Childears, Linda. "The Evolution of Young Americans and the Vision of Its Founder, Bill Daniels," October 25, 2010, presentation; Bradley, Dale. (2007). *The Future Begins Here: A Celebration of Your 20 Years at Young Americans*. The Daniels Fund.

Bill gives bank customers $100 on first-year anniversary and descriptions of early loans: Martin, Claire. "Small Investors." *Continental Profiles*, 2(8), August 1989.

Young entrepreneur interview on the *Today* show: Singular, Stephen. (2003). *Relentless: Bill Daniels and the Triumph of Cable TV*. The Bill Daniels Estate, p. 294.

Current bank products: Young Americans Bank website: www.yacenter.org/young-americans-bank.

Success was not measured by the bottom line: Childears, Linda. "The Evolution of Young Americans and the Vision of Its Founder, Bill Daniels," October 25, 2010, presentation.

Fifth-year account statistics and accounts in 50 states and foreign countries: Booklet about Young Americans Bank, 2007. Bradley, Dale. (2007). *The Future Begins Here: A Celebration of Your 20 Years at Young Americans*. The Daniels Fund.

Young Americans Education Foundation, Young AmeriTowne: Childears, Linda. "The Evolution of Young Americans and the Vision of Its Founder, Bill Daniels," October 25, 2010, presentation; Young Americans Center for Financial Education website: www.yacenter.org.

Bill's transfer of bank stock, federal regulations, creation of Young Americans Center for Financial Education, and funding the bank since Bill's death: "2011 Request for Bank and Program Support" from the Young Americans Center for Financial Education" to Daniels Fund Board of Directors, November 16, 2010; Interview with Linda Childears, November 3, 2011; "Preserving Donor Intent," August 2008, Daniels Fund unpublished document; "Young Americans Policy," August 2009, Daniels Fund unpublished document.

Bill is most proud of Young Americans Bank: "Young Americans Policy," August 2009, Daniels Fund unpublished document.